The Road Back

The Road Back

Norman C. Hill

Bookcraft
Salt Lake City, Utah

Library of Congress Catalog Card Number: 89-83388

ISBN 0-88494-717-3

First Printing, 1989

Printed in the United States of America

In many of the stories included in this book, names and locations of people involved have been changed to maintain their preferred anonymity.

Contents

1

Repentance: A Beginning

All of us make mistakes. We have problems. We commit sins. We might readily admit to anyone who would inquire that we are not perfect. Yet despite our willingness to acknowledge imperfections, generally it is much more difficult to itemize and confess our sins individually. Why? What holds us back from acknowledging our individual shortcomings one by one? Does it seem old-fashioned? Has too much emphasis on repentance in Primary and youth programs made it seem like something we do only when growing up? Or do we believe it is reserved just for those who commit serious transgressions? On the other hand, sometimes all we may see *is* our sins, our imperfections, the distance between the person we each want to be and the person we are. Despite our best efforts, we may feel that we are terribly unworthy of even the smallest of the Lord's blessings.

As we search for the right balance, avoiding both self-justification for our sins and excessive self-effacement due to our imperfections, the experience of others can guide us. Where have others tossed and turned, struggled, and found comfort and direction? Where are the blind alleys, the detours, the paths which look promising but lead nowhere? More important, where is the path that, though it may not appear well worn, is nonetheless well traveled and leads eventually to hope, safety, and eternal life?

The stories in this book, all true, are about the hopes, worries, concerns, and spiritual aspirations of faithful Latter-day Saints who are trying to live the gospel as well as they know how. These people are not perfect. They have made mistakes. They have committed sins, some of which have been serious enough violations of Church standards to warrant Church courts. However, most of the people in these stories describe their more ordinary struggles with the very real day-to-day problems which have limited their spiritual growth. They have been willing to share their personal experiences in the hope that others might be able to relate to the repentance process they have experienced and thereby realize their own "miracle of forgiveness."

Repentance, while not easy, is a process that each of us can learn. We should not make it more difficult than it is. It may be an arduous struggle to decide to repent, to get to the point of embarking on this process of changing our lives. But once we have made that choice, repentance itself is a relatively simple procedure which will allow us such peace that our having to go through the process will seem well worth the effort. The scriptures give this definition of repentance: "By this ye may know if a man repenteth of his sins—behold, he will confess them and forsake them" (D&C 58:43).

Confess and *forsake.* The dictionary defines the word *confess* as "to acknowledge or disclose; to admit." To confess our sins, then, is to acknowledge them and hold them up for examination so we can see them for what they are. But to whom do we confess or admit our sins? We always confess our sins directly to the Lord in our prayers. In addition, for certain transgressions a bishop is the Lord's authorized agent to hear an acknowledgment of sin. In all cases, of course, we must admit to ourselves that we have sinned and then make a decision to do something about it. The scriptures record that we tend to "cover our sins"—to hide them, to justify them, to give ourselves excuses for not doing something about them. Without confessing or acknowledging our sins, we cannot forsake them. After all, if we won't even admit or acknowledge a sin for what it is, how can we begin to do anything about it?

Forsake, too, appears to be a term well chosen in the scriptures. To forsake something is to leave it behind, to forget it, to ignore it as if it were never there. The Lord told Abraham to forsake the land of his birth and the strange gods who were worshipped there. The Lord also told Abraham he would receive a new land and a new name to symbolize his commitment to the Lord. Repentance is not a report card keeping track of our achievements and failures and grading us for our performance. It is instead a refining fire that helps us get rid of everything that is not us, everything that distorts, dilutes, clutters, or compromises the eternal person each of us is.

It may well be that sins are not only offensive to the Lord but also physically destructive and unhealthy to us. Books such as *Love, Medicine, and Miracles* and *Anatomy of an Illness as Perceived by a Patient* have documented the connection between positive attributes and physical health. After reviewing evidence on this matter, Rabbi Harold Kushner wrote:

> In the same way that the human body is fashioned so that certain foods and certain kinds of activity are healthier for us than others, I believe that God made the human soul in such a way that certain kinds of behavior are healthier for us than others. Jealousy, selfishness, mistrust poison the soul; honesty, generosity, and cheerfulness restore it. We literally feel better after we have gone out of our way to be helpful to someone. (*When All You've Ever Wanted Isn't Enough* [New York: Summit Books, 1986], p. 182.)

Repentance is good for us in many ways. It helps us see ourselves as we truly are, not just the way the world sees us. If we forsake our sins, the Lord will not only forgive us but he will also acknowledge our willingness to try. Only the Lord sees into our hearts and notices the angry words we did not say, the temptations we resisted, and the patience and perseverance little noticed and long forgotten by those around us.

Although the way to repentance is clear-cut, the path is not always easy. The ordinary tasks of day-to-day living can distract us. Routine and necessary tasks—busyness—can sometimes appear to be all there is time for. Balance is difficult. But failing to examine our lives, our actions, our aspirations, prevents us from realizing the best within us. Only through self-examination can we see our sins for what they really are: the baggage of this world, which, like a heavy winter coat in a sunny Caribbean clime, is unnecessary and burdensome.

In Hosea 10:12 the prophet instructs the people: "Sow to yourselves in righteousness, reap in mercy; break up your fallow ground: for it is time to seek the Lord." Fallow or unplowed ground is crusty and hard, overgrown with weeds. It cannot be planted with life-renewing seeds until it is turned over and broken up. If we are preoccupied with the things of this world, if our commitment to Church ordinances and charitable service is half-hearted, if we persist in playing games with sin; then even sincere attempts to change and improve our lives will fall short. We must do more than grit our teeth and make New Year's resolutions. Repentance is more than behavioral change. It is turning from sin and turning to the Lord. It demands that we plow some fallow ground in our lives.

It can be difficult to confront our sins and see them for what they are. Many, in fact, don't even like to use the word *sin* anymore. They prefer words which don't seem so harsh. If our sins are merely minor "flaws" then it is easier to pass them off as not being so bad and thereby avoid doing anything about them. Rationalization is easier if we can gloss over our "shortcomings."

If we take the time to examine who we are, what we believe in, and what we really think life is all about, however, it is easier to stop playing games with sin. Simply taking the time to ask questions about our thoughts and actions can improve our spirituality. Backbiting, jealousy, pride, anger, lying, selfishness, impure thoughts, and other sins will be reduced simply by our being more aware of their frequency and usage in our lives.

Those who know us well, or think they do, can also deter us from forsaking our sins. In his play *Murder in the Cathedral*, T.S. Eliot portrays the dilemma of Thomas

Becket. One interpretation of the theme of this play emphasizes that, after years of doing the bidding of King Henry II of England, Becket is made archbishop of Canterbury in a clever scheme to provide official justification for the king's unholy acts. With time, however, Becket responds to spiritual promptings and refuses to speak in Henry's behalf. Eventually Becket is visited by separate messengers from the king. The first urges Becket to publicly exonerate Henry so Becket will be able to continue doing good for the church. The second messenger advises Becket to say nothing against the king, but to let the people judge the king's acts for themselves.

The final messenger takes a different approach. He questions Becket's motives and taunts him by accusing him of trying to improve his competitive position in the next life by condemning others in this life. As this messenger leaves, Becket searches his own heart to understand his motives. Eventually, when Becket acts, he does so out of a desire to do well regardless of what others may say or how they may judge his actions.

There are many who would question our motives when we attempt to do well. We may even be our own worst accusers, seeing our faults more clearly than our virtues. President David O. McKay advised Church members to focus on specific habits, thoughts, or actions in turning from sin. He noted that in the morning hours, before our minds are cluttered with the cares of the day, we are especially receptive to inspiration and should use a few minutes each day for self-assessment. During such moments we can examine our motives and clarify our own course of action.

At such times, we may not always have specific answers to the questions that may trouble us, such as "Why me?" or "Why this?" or "How can I overcome this?'' But knowing the grand ''why'' of life will help us endure the gritty everyday problems and temptations that come our way. We can turn away from the influences of this world and yield to the promptings of the Spirit. We can change. We know we can. We simply need to decide that nothing else matters nearly so much. Nothing!

There is perhaps no greater need in the world today than the need for repentance. We have, in fact, been counseled to ''say nothing but repentance unto this generation'' (D&C 6:9). President Spencer W. Kimball wrote: ''There is a prevalent, perhaps subconscious, feeling that the Lord designed repentance only for those who commit murder or adultery or theft or other heinous crimes. This is of course not so. If we are humble and desirous of living the gospel we will come to think of repentance as applying to everything we do in life, whether it be spiritual or temporal in nature.'' (*The Miracle of Forgiveness* [Salt Lake City: Bookcraft, 1969], pp. 32–33.) Repentance is a positive message, a rewarding solution. It is at the heart of the gospel of Jesus Christ, the purpose of which, as David O. McKay stated, is ''to make evil-minded men and women good, and to make good men and women better'' (in Conference Report, October 1958, p. 94).

2

You Can Go Home Again

Raymond arrived home early that night. He had been traveling on business quite a bit lately and usually drove straight from the airport to the office before coming home. I teased him a little about being home in the middle of the day, especially since he had a high council meeting that night. He said somewhat ominously that that was why he was home early and that we needed to talk privately. As I searched his face for clues, it became apparent that something was really wrong.

When we were alone in the bedroom, Raymond sat down beside me on the edge of the bed without looking at me. He began slowly, his eyes riveted to the floor. "I need to talk to the stake president tonight," he said, "about me. I've committed a moral infraction. Since I'm on the high council there will probably be a Church court, and I'll likely be excommunicated."

I was bewildered, disoriented, and uncertain. I didn't know whether to slap his face or put my arms around him. I wanted to do both. I tried to think of the proper response. How should I handle this? But there was nothing I could recall from any Relief Society lesson or scripture study to help me. I was on my own.

After Raymond left for his meeting, I sat in my well-used wooden rocking chair. It always gave me a certain sense of security to sit in that familiar chair where I had comforted each of our five children when they were babies. Now who would comfort me? Who would caress my forehead and reassure me that everything would be all right?

How should I react? What was I supposed to do now? I wasn't particularly upset or angry so much as I was unable to figure out what to do next. I liked things neat and orderly in my life. I didn't like surprises or uncertainty. Now I had one more complication to deal with on an already full slate of activities, and I didn't have room for it.

As I sat and rocked and thought about the situation my first reaction was to minimize what had happened. *So what?* I thought. *What's so bad about what he's done? It's not like he's had an ongoing affair. He made a mistake, that's all. People make mistakes all the time. No big deal. Don't make this into something bigger than it is.* With pornography everywhere and Raymond covering five states in his sales territory, it was understandable that he could make a mistake like that. In fact, what was surprising was that it had not occurred sooner.

This initial reaction slowly yielded to another realization. If Raymond was excommunicated, everyone in the world would know about it. What would they think about us then? Would they think it was my fault? Would we be used in future Sunday School lessons as examples of what can happen if a couple doesn't maintain a strong marriage? I didn't want to be someone's object lesson! *Why did you do this to me, Raymond?* I thought. *You . . . you. . . .* Now the private marital problems we had been having would be on public display. Now the whole world would see that we had not been getting along all that well for the last few years.

I've always wanted to be admired and respected by those who know me. As stake Primary president I had seen significant progress in the programs and activities, and I had seen positive results of the stake's work with the children. Would people look down on me now? Would I still be listened to? Or would I be seen as a "bad wife" who wasn't available enough for her husband? I wondered and worried.

I went to the sink to splash water on my tired eyes. As I gazed into the mirror, I was startled by another thought. What if we were assigned special home teachers? Worse, what if someone decided on their own to use us as their reclamation project? I didn't want to be singled out and catered to! Now I was angry, and nothing had even happened yet.

I was getting all worked up and anxious over the possible reactions of others that had not even occurred. I was focusing *outward* on what others thought rather than *inward* on how to deal with the problem that confronted both Raymond and me.

I'm not going to take responsibility for this, I told myself. *This is his problem and not mine. No one can make me feel guilty about it.* But *I* had a problem too. How was I going to react to and cope with the aftermath of his sin? Then and there, I knelt in prayer and asked the Lord for strength to steer a steady course through the approaching storm. I was in uncharted waters and I knew it. Such emergencies have an uncanny way of focusing attention on what's really important. Suddenly a whole host of things didn't seem to matter very much after all.

Within weeks a high council court was held and Raymond was excommunicated. He went to church the following Sunday as he always had and was there during priesthood meeting when the bishop announced that Raymond had lost his Church membership. I was proud of him for attending priesthood meeting that day rather than finding a reason to stay at home. Knowing that he was bearing the shame of his transgression made it easier for me to bear it too. Later that day we talked to our children, since they were old enough to understand what had happened. No words can adequately describe how difficult it is to tell your own children about something like this. To look at their faces and recall past family home evening lessons on avoiding the evil influences of the world and then to admit that a parent has given in to such a temptation is awful. Still, Raymond was the patriarch of our family. He was still our dad. That hadn't changed.

Now I was bitter. And angry. I could prevent many unwanted influences in our home, but I could not control the loss of their innocence that went with trying to help the children understand why their father could no longer take the sacrament or pray in church or wear temple garments.

Growing up, I had dreamed of a perfect husband, a perfect marriage, and an eternal relationship. I wanted it to be so and was willing to do my part to make it so. Through the years, when Raymond and I were having difficulties I could always pass them off as normal marital conflicts. Not anymore. Now I had to confront them face to face. There was no other way.

Later that night Raymond asked me if I wanted a divorce. It was the first time the subject had ever come up. At age forty-one, with five children, I considered divorce as unthinkable then as the excommunication of my husband had been less than a month ago. It simply was something I never considered.

What I was now forced to examine was a marriage which was less than ideal. Would we ever be able to have the kind of life that I read about in the *Ensign* and heard about at general conference? Did we have the ability to measure up spiritually? By nature, I didn't like to talk openly about my feelings. It didn't feel comfortable to me, seemed almost like wearing someone else's shoes. I'd rather do almost anything else than talk about my feelings.

But Raymond felt it was important to try to talk things out. He needed it. I told him I would participate on two conditions: I wanted no details of what he had done or why he had done it, and I wanted to deal with the present and the future, not the past. He agreed. So for the next six months Raymond and I talked a lot about our feelings. Sometimes we would select a topic or question for an evening's discussion and write separate answers to it on a notepad, and then we would explain our answers. On successive nights we discussed such topics as:

— How do I feel about you right now?
— How do I think you feel about me right now?
— What things are most important in my life?
— What things do we spend a lot of time doing which are not important?
— Is our marriage worth keeping?
— What makes me lose my temper and get angry?
— What makes me happy?
— What makes me sad?
— Why do I react the way I do to some of the things you say?

Sometimes Raymond would talk most of the night. It was important to him to probe and question and follow up on everything I said. I didn't realize it then, but I think he was trying to determine whether I was just going to put up with him for the rest of my life or whether I was willing to forgive him and rebuild our life together. I wasn't sure myself. I wanted to get on with things—cleaning the house, taking care of the children, leading the Primary. I didn't know what I felt about Raymond or about the overwhelming questions for which he wanted answers. I did my best to be responsive, but it didn't come easily for me.

I tried not to act differently at church even though I speculated that some people were whispering about me behind my back. I pretended that nothing had happened and I did the things I had always done—lingering in the halls chatting after meetings, making a fuss over the new babies born in the ward, teaching a miniclass in Relief Society. And because I acted the same, people treated me the same way they always had.

Below the surface, though, Raymond and I were troubled. Twice, while he was away on a business trip, he phoned and said he could not go on. He was so despondent that I had to fly to the city where he was and bring him home. During this time he was meeting regularly with the bishop, the stake president, and an LDS Social Services counselor. There were others, too, who were providing as much emotional support as possible.

But I felt spiritually and emotionally drained. And who was there for me? Where were my counselors? I was experiencing as much trauma as Raymond was, but who was helping me? Didn't others know that I had to carry this man? I was irritated with my local leaders for not recognizing that I had counseling needs too. I wanted to talk to somebody but I didn't know how to approach them about it. That was a mistake. I should have found a way.

So I turned to the only resource I could turn to. I turned to the Lord. In my loneliness and frustration and despair, I told the Lord that I needed help just to cope. I didn't ask for a miracle. I didn't ask him to change Raymond. I didn't even ask to make things better or to help me feel better, I just asked the Lord to help me cope. I just wanted to make it through the day.

At times I would feel so discouraged that I would offer this same prayer several times a day. I was under a great deal of stress with everyone depending on me and no one being there for me to lean on. I didn't feel that I deserved what was happening, but nonetheless I had to deal with it. I didn't hold anything in particular against Raymond. I saw him as a person who thought he was more resistant to temptation than he actually was. Because I understood that about him I wasn't jealous or resentful about what he had done, even though that didn't make it any easier to deal with my personal reaction to his actions.

So I took each day at a time. I didn't expect too much too soon. I didn't try to put up a front at church, but I didn't act like a martyr either. I think it helped to be part of a group—a ward, a Relief Society—and to know that I was valued for the good qualities I had. Just doing the ordinary, mundane things of life helped too by providing a sense of balance.

While some things did get better, others got worse. Raymond lost his job. Reluctantly we relocated and started anew somewhere else.

It was an odd feeling when we stood and had our membership records read during sacrament meeting in our new ward. It was strange to have everyone but Raymond stand at the appropriate time. We told the bishopric that Raymond could not participate in public prayers or certain other activities, but we didn't tell anyone else in the ward. Occasionally Raymond would be called upon by a class teacher to give a prayer, and I would pretend they had said Sister Anderson rather than Brother Anderson. He did participate as much as he could—as a basketball coach and as Scout merit badge counselor. Life does go on, and time does heal many wounds. As the weeks stretched into months, we again reestablished the ordinary routine of our lives. There is a certain appeal in knowing what you're going to do tomorrow and the next day and the day after.

As time passed, I tried to leave these events in the past. I didn't want to be Raymond's advocate or his accuser. I just wanted to leave the past alone. But I could not. There was too much unfinished business. Until I could better resolve my feelings toward him, I knew I couldn't go on. Regardless of how much I didn't want to think about it, I had to come face-to-face with myself. I had to put aside my craving to be "accepted," my tendency to deal superficially, and I had to find a way to go forward. I didn't consider myself any kind of great example of how to do this, but I think it helped a lot just to say, "Okay, this is it. It happened to me, not someone else. I didn't want it this way, but this is the way it is. So what?" And in saying "So what?" all my pretensions, all my put-ons, and all my keeping a stiff upper lip came tumbling down. When I saw myself, really saw myself, it helped me see Raymond in a whole new light. He was no longer the person who had hurt me and changed my world. He was instead a person with weaknesses who needed help. Just like me.

After several years of determined effort and through the efforts of a good bishop, the necessary papers were prepared for Raymond to be rebaptized. As part of the process, Raymond asked me to write a letter indicating whether or not I had forgiven him.

As I began to write the letter, a variety of impressions came to mind. *Oh, this will sound convincing,* I remember thinking as I wrote one paragraph. *Raymond will like this,* I thought about another paragraph, anticipating that it would be a boost to his self-esteem and personal commitment when he read it. But did I believe it? Was I just saying things I thought others wanted to hear, or had I truly forgiven Raymond?

I put down my pen and gazed out the window. *This isn't a game,* I thought. *This is as real as anything that exists in this life or the next.* I couldn't fake it. But I was still uncertain. Had the scars healed? Had I truly let go of all the hurt? Why did I have to deal with such impossible questions anyway?

I searched for some way to get a perspective on my true feelings. I didn't want to be superficial or to simply make up things to say. I read the scriptures searching for inspiration or maybe a passage to quote, but nothing seemed quite right. I looked in my journal hoping some incident or memory would guide my thoughts. As I read my recollections about our life together I was struck by how much I had been loved by members of the Church wherever I had lived. No matter what I was going through, I had never felt rejected or excluded. There was always a place for me, always ample space in others' hearts for me and my family. No one had ever put out a "no vacancy" sign for us. I wanted that for Raymond too. With that in mind, it was now easier to say how I had changed and forgiven him.

Two years after Raymond was rebaptized, we moved back to the ward in Portland where all of this had started. Like a timid child on her first day at school,

I worried about what people would think about *me* and about Raymond. Would it be like standing in a crowded elevator with a group of strangers? Would we be accepted or would there be some hesitation? We had felt loved there before; would we feel it again? As I nervously went to church that first Sunday, I looked into the eyes of each person who greeted us. But there was no hesitation anywhere that day in the eyes I saw; there was no looking down at shoes or looking away at imaginary objects. People seemed to just look inside as they said sincerely, "We're glad you're back."

Although I believe church callings are simply an opportunity to serve and not a sign of righteousness, I knew we had come home when several weeks later Raymond was called to the high council once again and I was called as stake Young Women's president. We never were unaccepted. It was as though we never really left home.

3

Charity Is Not Easily Provoked

The stake men's basketball championship game was about to begin. The referee reminded all of us that he was not a professional and urged us to consider that good sportsmanship was more important than winning. After a prayer, play began.

The score of the game seesawed back and forth as the game progressed. As the end of the game approached, the intensity of the players increased. To get an edge, players from both teams began to push and shove for positions near the basket. Finally, on an inbound play under our own basket, I called to the referee, "Hey, John, we're all getting tired and need you to call more fouls to keep us honest."

The fellow in the other ward who was guarding me was offended by my remark. "C'mon, you crybaby," he said, "play ball and leave the ref out of it." Startled, I threw the ball in and said nothing more.

On the next play, however, while getting into position for a rebound I felt two hands on my lower back and was pushed off balance. Then a moment later I was hit in the nose by an elbow. Since I was away from the ball both times, neither of the officials noticed what happened.

So that's the way you want to play, is it? I angrily said to myself. Though intentional fouling is not fair, I knew I could stick up for myself if it was not noticed by the referee. So I made a point of backing into my opponent and knocking him off balance during the next series of plays at his end of the court. Again, no foul was called. I could see that the opposing player was very agitated.

Then it happened. I had the ball on a fast break with no one between me and the basket except this same player who had been guarding me all night. As I went up for a shot, a forearm came down on the bridge of my nose and I went down hard to the floor. A foul was called, but I hardly heard the whistle as I jumped up and charged toward my opponent.

"C'mon, buddy, start something," he taunted.

"You're not worth it," I shot back. "Why don't you get some 'odor-eaters' for your mouth instead of your shoes?"

As we were separated, a player who served in the bishopric of the other ward grabbed me. "C'mon, Clint," he said. "What kind of example are you to the kids who are watching? I thought you were better than this."

"Leave me alone, Paul!" I said angrily. "Who made you my judge and jury? What makes you so righteous anyway? I don't want to be counseled when I'm bruised and bleeding."

"Give the guy a break, Clint," he replied. "He's just been coming back to activity in the Church. The referee called a foul on him. Take it easy, would you?"

Bruised and embarrassed, I didn't know what to say. So I turned and walked off the court and into the locker room. I gathered my things and walked slowly to my car. Once there, I rested my head on the steering wheel. Who was right and who was wrong? I didn't start it, he did. I was provoked.

The longer I sat alone in the car, however, the more confused I became. As I sat there, I remembered a talk I had given several months ago in sacrament meeting. "It doesn't matter who is right and who is wrong when you know someone is offended," I had said. "When you know someone is offended, you should do something about it." I even told the story of a good friend who was a bishop in a rural town in northern Utah. A disagreement had occurred between him and a neighbor over irrigation rights. Finally my friend privately went to three different members of the high council and related the facts of the incident as accurately as possible, and he asked each of them who was right and who was wrong. After asking a variety of questions, each high councilor said my friend was right and his neighbor was wrong. While two of these men advised that the matter should be dropped and would soon be forgotten, the third advised that my friend should go to his neighbor and apologize.

"But why?" he asked. "You said I was right and my neighbor was wrong. He should apologize to me."

"No, you don't understand. If you *recognize* that someone is offended, you should go to them and try to work out your differences."

"It would be hard to do," my friend replied. "I don't think I can do it. It would break my heart."

"Exactly," came the response. "Do you think when the scriptures refer to a 'broken heart and a contrite spirit' they mean to say it is easily obtained?"

I couldn't put the story out of my mind. I didn't want to rationalize or excuse or justify my actions. But I didn't want to be insincere, either. I was having a hard time avoiding the self-righteous feelings I would have inside if at that moment I walked back into the gym and apologized. "You don't have my sense of honor and so I have taken on the moral obligation of apologizing to you" were the words in my heart at that moment. Even if I didn't say those words, that is what I would mean. Regardless of whether or not anyone else knew it, I would know it.

So what should I do? Was doing nothing really the best course of action? Doing nothing at least meant avoiding hypocrisy. "Dear Lord, help me," I prayed. "I want to do the right thing, but I don't know what I should do. Help me, please."

I went back into the gym and sat with my team. When the game was over I made a point of shaking each player's hand on both teams, congratulating them, and saying simply, "I'm sorry I got mad on the court tonight."

The next day was Sunday. I felt better about myself for not letting the incident go without some kind of reconciliation with the other ward and those I had shouted at. But I still felt bad inside. Why had I reacted angrily in the first place? After all, it was only a basketball game.

I had my priesthood lesson for the deacons prepared, so I simply reviewed the main points while the prelude music was being played. But I was interrupted by two of my deacons. "You had a right to get mad at that guy, Brother Davis. We could see him hanging on you all night." Startled, I didn't know what to say as they walked past me to take their seats. Then a father of one of the priests slid in beside me. "My son Tommy told me about the game last night. He said he was surprised that a quiet guy like you could get angry at all. I guess it builds up sometimes and you just have to let it out, right, Clint?" Without waiting for a reply he leaned over to his counselor in the elders quorum presidency and started a conversation about home teaching.

I was starting to get irritated. I didn't want one more person to say something to me about the game last night. I wanted it simply to be forgotten. I didn't want to be reminded of it or to have to defend my actions or apologize for them. But when the bishop called for a report on the game, Dan, our coach, almost seemed compelled to say something about it. He drew an analogy between my anger at Saturday's game and the anger of the Savior driving the money changers out of the temple in righteous indignation, and he commented on my refusal to be bullied by a larger player.

I sank lower in my seat. I was humiliated. Now I was becoming an object lesson! I didn't want to be a folk hero or a scapegoat for something I did wrong. I didn't want the incident rehearsed again and again like an instant replay feature of a football game on television. I didn't want others judging me one way or the other, to agree or disagree with my actions, to generalize that one mistake, one loss of temper, would inevitably lead to another; or to assume that because I was provoked I was fully justified in doing what I did. Unreasonably, I suppose, I wanted my public behavior to be a private matter.

I was irritated and upset when I arrived home from church. Three more people had stopped me in the hall to inquire about the incident. *It's being blown out of proportion,* I thought. *It's not fair. I tried to do the right thing after I got angry, but no one even seemed to notice what I did —and I'm sure not going to tell them. It just isn't fair.*

At home I perfunctorily played with my three small children while my wife fixed dinner, but all the while I was fuming inside. Afterwards, when we were alone, my wife asked what was wrong and we talked again about the incident and about ward members' reactions to it and questions about it.

"Others are wrong for even bringing it up. Whether they thought you were right or wrong, it is none of their business," she said. "And you're wrong for being so sensitive to them."

"Thanks for the sympathy," I coolly replied. "If I ever need help again, I'll keep you in mind."

"I don't think you should go around blaming others and making it seem as if you're doing your best in spite of them," she calmly responded. "You felt you were wrong by getting angry *regardless* of whether or not you were provoked. Until you've fully resolved that matter to *your* satisfaction, you won't feel right. Don't let rationalizations and accusing feelings serve as a substitute for complete reconciliation of the incident."

And with that she left the room. It was the best thing she could have done. My conscience said she was correct, that I was more concerned about what others in the ward thought of me, about my reputation with them, than I was about pursuing goodness for its own sake. If she had stayed, my ego and pride would not have let me admit that to her. However, at that moment I wasn't about to give up my hurt and angry feelings in favor of people who I was convinced didn't deserve to be treated better. I sat there thinking, *I will be civil and polite to others, but not kind. I'll guard my own feelings carefully and avoid showing any emotions whatsoever: joy or anger, mercy or sorrow.* An almost unwitting ruthlessness seemed to come over me.

During the next few weeks I tried to put the incident behind me. Work demands absorbed my time and concentration during the week, and Boy Scouts' and deacons' activities filled in the spaces left over. But I wasn't happy. I was melancholy, restless, troubled. Everyone and everything seemed to get on my nerves. When I was about to leave for a youth activity my wife asked me to pick up some milk on my way home. I did, but later when I arrived home I found that I had left my wallet at the store. Angrily I scolded her for giving me so many little things to do that I could not keep things straight.

Everything in our family seemed strained. A few days later when we were driving to a movie together, a commotion started in the backseat.

"Ryan's looking out *my* window," my ten-year-old daughter said.

"He's in the middle. What else can he do?" I replied.

"I don't look out *his* window when I'm in the middle," she responded.

At this point I stopped the car and spun around in my seat. "Well, let's just poke Ryan's eyes out then. Let's get a stick and blind him so that he *never* looks out *your* window again. Will that make you happy? Will you be satisfied then?"

Without waiting for an answer, I threw open my door and jerked him out of the car into the street. While holding him tightly at the elbow, I searched the side of the road until I found a large, pointed stick. Gripping it with whitened knuckles, I raised it high over my head. By this time my son was frantically struggling to free himself, my daughter was in tears, and my wife was coldly staring at me. I tossed the stick aside and in oppressive silence drove to the theater. At that moment I felt almost justified in giving them a scare. I wouldn't have poked my own son's eyes out, of course.

I sat alone that night in the living room when everyone else had gone to bed. Who was I really? What was I becoming? I seemed to wallow in self-righteous pity one moment and in shallow, childish behavior the next. Were my attempts at righteous thoughts and deeds mere facades and pretensions? Maybe those who thought I was fatally flawed were right. Maybe I was not so good after all. Maybe I just couldn't help being the way that I was.

As I sat there rocking, I realized how insecure I was becoming—doubtful, uncertain, anxious, and completely preoccupied with myself, who I was, what I might have been. If sin is bondage, then surely self-doubt is the jailer and personal preoccupation the warden.

So what could I do about it? I pulled my scriptures from the bookcase, turned to the Topical Guide, and began reading all the references under the heading "Sin." Two different passages impressed me: Alma's advice to his son, Corianton, and Nephi's counsel to his brethren.

> And now, my son, I desire that ye should let these things trouble you no more, and only let your sins trouble you, with that trouble which shall bring you down unto repentance.
>
> O my son, I desire that ye should deny the justice of God no more. Do not endeavor to excuse yourself in the least point because of your sins, by denying the justice of God; but do you let the justice of God, and his mercy, and his long-suffering have full sway in your heart; and let it bring you down to the dust in humility. (Alma 42:29–30.)

> And now, my beloved brethren, seeing that our merciful God has given us so great knowledge

> concerning these things, let us remember him, and lay aside our sins, and not hang down our heads, for we are not cast off (2 Nephi 10:20).

Was it that easy? Was it simply a matter of recognizing the accusations I was making of myself in my heart, avoiding justifying either my self-righteous inclinations or my base emotional reactions, and then calling upon Christ with the feeling that I was more interested in what he would have me do than in what I felt I deserved from others? Could it be?

I found a pencil and paper. I wrote down as many good characteristics of myself as I could think of. I was good! The angry, resentful feelings I had experienced the past few weeks weren't the real me. Next I tried to record the times when I had expressed anger towards others—and why I thought it was okay at the time to do so. When I wrote down my reasons, they looked pretty silly. I knelt to pray. I asked the Lord if he would help bear my burden, take my yoke upon his shoulders, help me break this self-perpetual cycle of anger, blame, excuses, and self-doubt. Would he help me have enough faith in his power to do this?

As I stood up from this prayer I felt like a claustrophobic coming out of an elevator. I walked outside with the paper on which I had earlier written the list. Lighting a match to it, I watched it burn. "It was a list made by someone else," I said, "and I have no need for it."

4

Twists and Turns in the Road

Life is much different in the rural South today than it was at the turn of the century when I was a little girl. Back then, cotton was king and the boll weevil was still a long way off. In 1907, the year I was baptized as an eight-year-old, the railroad came to my hometown. It was a single-gauge track that ran along the edge of Tylertown connecting it with other towns in southern Mississippi. Tylertown was incorporated as a city later that same year and the elementary school classes my father taught moved into the old Hall Building just east of Magee's Creek. We had fewer than twenty students who could attend regularly during the morning hours that year, which meant it wasn't very crowded since we had two separate rooms near the back stairs on the second floor.

My parents and five older brothers and sisters had all been baptized four years earlier so I was the only person baptized that day. We had a pond behind the house where the missionaries sang some songs and asked me to recite as many of the Articles of Faith as I could recall. I needed help on some of the longer ones but finally finished them all. I was so proud of myself.

I was too young to know then that as a young black girl I was doing something that would alienate me from my neighbors. In Waltham County the black community attended the Mount Moriah Baptist Church and the white community attended the New Zion Baptist Church. There wasn't a middle ground. So when John Israel, a Mormon, and his family moved to Tylertown and eventually taught my father the gospel he was doing more than bringing a strange new religion to our area. By encouraging a black family to attend a "white" church, he was upsetting the entire social fabric of our community. And some of them let us know about it.

I remember that when I was ten or eleven I went to town with Mama and a group of white teenagers called us names and said we were "putting on airs" going to a "white" church. They said we ought to stay in our place or somebody might get hurt. I was worried that there would be some trouble right there until a shopkeeper, Warren Ryals, came outside and settled things down. I found out later that my father rode his horse over to Mr. Ryals's house that night and thanked him for doing something about the situation. A few weeks later some of the deacons from Mount Moriah Baptist Church called on my father to try to talk him out of taking his family to the Mormon Church. I overheard them talking while listening from my bedroom. They said that there were good relations between the black and white communities which didn't need to be upset. My father said that he was going to practice his faith regardless of what anyone else thought about it. He said he wasn't trying to make any kind of statement or pick a fight, he simply wanted to do the right thing according to the principles of the restored gospel.

There wasn't an organized branch of the Church in Tylertown, so we would usually study the scriptures by ourselves at home on Sundays. Sometimes we would meet with the Israels, but they moved when I was a teenager and I don't remember meeting with them very often. The missionaries came down when they could, and we would go to conference at Darbon, Mississippi, whenever it was held. It was a long ride by horse and buggy, especially since my parents made all the younger children wait outside on the lawn so we wouldn't disturb anyone trying to listen to the conference message. Oh, how we enjoyed the trip back home as Father retold the stories he had heard that day!

My father has always considered the principle of tithing as a matter of utmost importance. During the years he was a teacher, he never failed to send his tithing in a letter to the branch president in Darbon on the day he was paid. Later, when he farmed full-time, he would take a wagon load of goods to Darbon in the spring and in the fall when his vegetables were ready, giving them to the branch president in order to fulfill his obligation to the Lord.

As I grew older, even though I lived by all the gospel principles my parents taught me, I worried that I might never marry if I expected to find someone who was a member of the Church. Despite my parents' insisting that I not compromise my values, by the time I was twenty-one I was so desperate that I accepted a proposal from a New Orleans man with three children. He had never heard of the Mormons. We moved to New Orleans where I hoped I could teach him about the Church. But he was uncomfortable with the missionaries in our home and didn't like the teasing from our neighbors about his wife attending a "white" church. After two years he told me I could not go to church anymore, and he would not let me pay tithing on the money I earned from being a part-time seamstress.

I pleaded with him. I begged. I cried. But he would not change his mind. So I stopped going to church and didn't read the scriptures anymore for a time.

But I wouldn't stop setting aside my tithe. Since all my customers paid me in cash, I secretly took 10 percent and hid it in a trunk in the attic. I didn't make much money, but I knew that I could not give to anyone else what belonged to the Lord. Even though my life was not what I wanted it to be, I would not turn away from living the principle of tithing.

Without the Church, I didn't know where to turn for support or direction. My husband started drinking heavily and would sometimes not come home for several days. Then one night, after ten difficult years and after the children were all grown, he didn't come home at all.

I was relieved—and scared. What would I do now? How could I turn back to the Lord when I had deserted him for eight long years? Now that I was in trouble, how could I ask for help? It wasn't that I was too proud to ask for help; it just didn't seem right.

I wrote to my mother and father and told them my husband had left me. I said I had not been active in the Church for some time. I told them that I had to work something out on my own before I could see them again. I didn't want to be like the prodigal son who returned to his father's house, it seemed to me, simply because he knew there was a warm bed and a full meal available there.

One evening about three weeks later there was a knock on my door. I opened it to see my father and mother standing in a New Orleans rain next to the buckboard wagon. "We've come to take you home," they said. "You don't have to come, but we didn't want you to think you had to pass any test before you felt welcome."

We finished packing everything the next day—including the trunk with my tithing in it. Tears came to my daddy's eyes when he saw that I had put aside 10 percent of all the money I had ever earned since being married.

In 1938, I married again, this time to a God-fearing man who knew and understood my convictions and encouraged me to live by them. Although he was not at that time a Latter-day Saint, he took me to church and participated in Sunday School and sacrament meeting. We moved back to New Orleans to find work, which wasn't easy to locate because of the Great Depression. Rudolph had always played in a band just for fun in Mississippi and eventually was employed as a background musician for one of the big hotels in New Orleans.

Sometimes I would get discouraged because I could not fully participate in the activities of the Church. One night in anger I told the Lord that it wasn't fair that black people had to go to the back doors of white people's houses, could not eat their meal until others had finished, and had to call every white person Mr. and Miss even if the child was too young to talk. How could that be right? It was Christmastime 1946, and I just didn't feel very thankful for anything. That Christmas Rudolph gave me a copy of the book *Temples of the Most High* because a friend at church had recommended it to him. He didn't read well but he enjoyed having me read to him.

I wanted to believe that the message in that book included me. But I knew it didn't; it surely wasn't meant for me. I could go only so far in the kingdom of God. I had to stay in my place.

In the months that followed I tried hard to reconcile myself to the Lord. So what if I couldn't have everything? Half a loaf was better than none. If things were not as good as I wished them to be, at least they were not as bad as some of my neighbors expected them to be. I lived quietly on the edge of Church activity, serving occasionally as a Relief Society visiting teacher and helping out with dinners on homemaking night.

I wanted something more. I wanted to give myself fully and completely to the gospel. I wanted to do some great deed. But I held back. Reluctant to be hurt, I sat on the back row and listened and learned without giving much in return. Unwilling to offend or embarrass anyone, I rarely took part in gospel discussions except at home with Rudolph.

My complacent world was changed in 1960. That was the year federal marshals enforced the integration of public schools in New Orleans. Suddenly white people who were kind and accommodating to me on the streetcar became tense whenever I spoke to them. My black neighbors asked me why I went across town to church and told me I should be content to just be who I was without being pretentious. But I was neither a rebel nor an accommodationist. I simply was trying to do right as God gave me the power to do right.

Or was I? If I withheld some portion of commitment from the Lord, could I say that my heart was right with him? If there was a willingness on my part to give only "so much" and no more when I prayed or pondered the scriptures, could I say that I was fully following the dictates of my own conscience? I needed to know for myself that being a Mormon was not for show. But could the Lord help me? Wasn't this simply my problem to work out in my own way?

I had committed no great sin, but I was badly in need of repentance and forgiveness—if it was available to me—and guidance. I didn't want to do the right things for the wrong reasons. I did not want to be double-minded. I was caught in a world of turmoil and upheaval for which I was ill-prepared.

So I prayed. I prayed to know what I should do and how I should act. I prayed to have the Lord tell me what to do. As I prayed I felt as if someone were in the room with me. I opened my eyes to see who was there but found I was still alone. I began to pray again only to have the same sensation return to me. As I continued praying I told the Lord that I didn't want to continue half in and half out of the Church. I wanted to be loved as his daughter and accepted as his child. Then into my mind and heart came a peace and a reassurance. As I vowed to return good for evil, kindness to those who would harm others, and patience to those who were full of rancor, I felt accepted of the Lord. To control myself I had to lay my head upon the couch I was kneeling beside. With no axe to grind, with no cause to support, I could "press forward through the mist of darkness, clinging to the rod of iron" (1 Nephi 8:24).

Though the next three years were turbulent—once a brick was thrown at me and another time a home teacher carried a shotgun in his truck for protection when visiting me—I was able to strengthen my testimony by not taking sides in a divided city. I had already taken a stand and needed no other person or place on which to bestow my allegiance.

I determined right then and there to patiently respond to the angry remarks of others. I decided to read the scriptures, focusing on ways the Savior responded whenever he was ridiculed. By understanding his character better, perhaps I would better emulate his example. As I did this "character study," one verse in particular made a strong impression on me. In speaking to his disciples, Jesus said: "Henceforth I call you not servants; for the servant knoweth not what his lord doeth: but I have called you friends; for all things that I have heard of my Father I have made known unto you" (John 15:15).

Friends. How remarkable! Rather than "sticking up for my rights" or "turning the other cheek" I could respond to those who were angry about the blacks' changing role in our city by being a friend. I tried hard to notice the discomfort others might have when they were around me and deal with it. Sometimes I simply noticed something unique about them and looked for a way to give a compliment. Sometimes extending a common courtesy helped; and sometimes, a bit of humor. Eventually I cared less about my "place" and more about the people around me. I saw some of the whites on the streetcar looking just as scared as I was. Their world was changing and they couldn't control it any more than I could.

Rudolph died in 1974—four years before we would have been able to go to the temple together. I received my own endowment and was sealed to Rudolph in the Washington Temple on July 21, 1978, less than two months after the revelation allowing blacks to hold the priesthood. I was seventy-nine years old; and that day was one of the most glorious days of my life.

I am convinced that if I had let my annoyances and frustrations build up years ago, I would never have been worthy to go to the temple when I was able to go. By turning to the Lord when I was troubled about my place in his kingdom, I was able to turn away from resentment and loneliness. By turning back I was able to go forward.

5

Letting Go of Grudges

My cousin, Todd, had just turned forty-six. Our families had lived next door while we were growing up and since we are about the same age we did a lot of things together back then. I would not say we were best friends, either then or now. He was just enough older than me and had enough different interests as we started into our teenage years that our family connection seemed more a matter to ignore than to recognize. Although we had ridden Grandpa's horse together down to Howard's slough to go swimming on most hot summer days when we were ten and twelve years old, a couple of years later we hardly spoke to each other even if we passed in the halls at school. We were just different.

Now he was dying. He had a nontreatable disease and had been sent home by his doctors to enjoy what comfort he could there. And since I had not talked to him much in the years since I went on a mission and he left to try his hand at being a hockey player in western Canada, I was trying to figure out what to say to him. I was flying in from Boston on a business trip and my dad had asked me to go by and see him. "Go see him," Dad said on the phone. "He's in a lot of pain and just likes to see and talk to people."

There are lots of things about growing up with Todd that I was trying to remember, things I once had tried to forget. It was hard enough for both of us to be teenagers in the sixties anyway; we could have used each other's help. Instead, our growing up spawned either indifference or contempt depending on the incidents during which our paths crossed.

Once, at a ward basketball game, he was pulled out of the game by the coach near the end of the game in a clutch situation in which our team needed the height and rebounding ability I had rather than his backcourt quickness and speed. It was bad enough that I was younger and taller than him anyway, but to so obviously substitute for him in such a situation hurt his pride and ego a great deal. I held my hand up to give him a "high five" as I ran in from the scorer's table. Instead of slapping it, he walked slowly to the end of the bench with his eyes down. A look of disgust covered his face. The game was eventually won due less to any rebounds I got than to the shooting of one of our other players. We all cheered our victory—all but Todd, who dressed hurriedly and then silently slipped out of the back door of the gym and walked home.

I didn't see him much during that next week until Friday night. I worked most weekends on his dad's farm and that evening I went to their barn to do a list of chores my uncle had left for me while he was at the stockyard. Todd was already there loading salt blocks for the cows from a pickup truck onto a wooden pallet. I greeted him, but when he said nothing in reply I started sweeping the floor of a granary bin. Suddenly, unexpectedly, Todd grabbed the broom from my hands.

"Why're you doing this first?" he said with a certain hard edge in his voice. "You can do this later. Go move those hay bales further inside the barn."

"Don't worry about it," I shot back. "I'll get to it. Give me the broom back."

"Go do it now," he said flatly, not moving a muscle. "This can wait."

"Leave me alone, I'll get to it," I replied determinedly. "You're not in charge of me."

"You think you're a tough guy, don't you?" There was practically no emotion in his voice, no inflection even in asking a question. He threw the broom to the hard cement floor. As I bent down to pick it up, he stepped on the handle. Angry and frustrated, I pushed him as hard as I could and straightened up to face him.

"Put your dukes up, big boy," he jeered. "Let's go after it."

"I don't want to fight you," I responded and started to turn and walk away. I saw a right cross coming soon enough that I was able to partially back away from it. But the left jab that followed was too quick and powerful for me to dodge. He hit me squarely on the end of my nose. Instantly a trickle of blood started down my face.

He stood stoically in a boxer's position in front of me. "Let's go after it," he repeated again flatly.

"I don't want to fight you. Leave me alone," I replied through clenched teeth. And he did. There was no taunting, no jeers; he never even brought the incident up again. He had wanted to prove a point and had gone about the job with determined resignation. Apparently it was something he had to do. He needed to reclaim his pride. With the task complete, he could go on with other things.

I couldn't. I resented his taking advantage of his strength and age to humiliate me. What had I ever done to him? What had I done to deserve getting smashed in the face? It may not have been much of an incident to Todd, but it was for me. *He may be able to forget it easily,* I thought months later, *but I cannot. It's not fair for him to take advantage of me like that.*

Time passed, but all was neither forgotten nor forgiven. From then on, I was never really comfortable around Todd. I felt I had to watch my step and be careful what I said or did with him. I wanted to distance myself from him in any way that I could. I felt taken advantage of, picked on because I was younger, for something that was not my fault. I resented him, and I let my grudge smolder without telling anyone about it. When something good happened to others his age and not to him or when something bad happened to him, I quietly gloated. I enjoyed his misfortunes.

After his graduation from high school Todd drifted. He went to college for a year but then dropped out. He tried to make it in the junior professional hockey circuit for a while but that too became such a grind that he soon returned home to the family farm.

Todd had stopped living basic gospel principles when he left home. Now, upon returning, he had no interest in shedding the bad habits he had picked up. He chewed tobacco, drank beer, used bad language, and ridiculed others for going on missions. He had little effect on me because of my resentment toward him.

After serving a mission I went away to college and then accepted out-of-state employment. I didn't think about Todd much. He wasn't an important person in my life. During the ensuing fifteen years, my parents would comment occasionally about the stormy life he led. In his early thirties Todd had eventually married but then divorced a few years later. His marriage had been unhappy to say the least.

I saw him occasionally when I returned for family reunions or visits with my parents. He was typically sullen, withdrawn, full of his own problems. In some of my church lessons, he became an unnamed object lesson, an example of a wasted life.

Then, on a short visit with my parents, I was surprised to discover that Todd's first wife's son by a previous marriage was living with him for the summer. He was about twelve and enjoyed the outdoors. I saw them together at a store and noticed something different in Todd, something I didn't think he was capable of—tenderness. They didn't see me watching them down an aisle when Todd fleetingly put his arm around his stepson's shoulder. Was this the same Todd? Was he really different?

"He *is* different," my parents said. "But he always had a good heart," they added, "and it's just showing through the crustiness he has built up over the years." I wasn't sure. Maybe it was an act. Maybe he was just lonely. Maybe he had some ulterior motive. I didn't think he had a good heart.

A year passed and I didn't think about Todd much at all. Then my dad told me Todd had gone to the doctor because he was having trouble breathing. After a series of tests, cancer was diagnosed. Various treatments were tried. None were successful. The doctors couldn't do anything more for him, they said. He was released from the hospital to go home. "However," my dad said excitedly, "he's going to church again!"

Going to church again? Why? *Now that he has an incurable disease he's going to church again*, was my first thought. *Deathbed repentance.* Or was it? Isn't it true that almost everyone who makes some type of major change is prompted to do so by a crisis? Who was I to judge Todd's motives anyway? What made me suddenly such an authority on his reasons for going back to church? And regardless of why he decided to change, wasn't the real issue his sincerity now? I ended this conversation with my dad with all these questions circling in my mind like airplanes at a busy airport.

That had been weeks ago. Now I was on my way to see him. I still had lots of unanswered questions about Todd—and some about me. I had always thought of myself as a positive, supportive person who was interested in the best for others. I had served in bishoprics and on high councils and had taught Sunday School classes in every age category. I had always wanted to touch people's lives positively and had felt good about helping others and giving what I thought was meaningful service. Now I wondered, was it a sham? Was I only able to feel empathy and compassion for certain people and not for someone in my extended family? "But he hurt me on purpose," I said out loud to no one in particular. I didn't want to rationalize my negative feelings, but I didn't want my own sensitive nature to make me take the blame for something that was not my fault, either.

I spent almost an hour with Todd. We talked about a lot of things, mostly trivial topics like the weather and hockey teams. There were some long pauses and occasionally some strained laughter in our conversation. He was in a lot of pain so I didn't joke around much. His face showed it the most through deep grimaces and a furrowed brow that made me realize how much older he looked than me. But he was different than I remembered. Gone was the resentment toward others, the chip on his shoulder that I remembered. He was subdued, quieter, and showed an interest in hearing what others had to say rather than exhibiting the silent indifference and smoldering animosity which had previously been his trademark. He was not the same person I had expected. Not without his biases and prejudices, he talked about how pushy some people were in the Northeast—but he was different nonetheless.

I went home still wondering whether Todd's change was prompted solely by his disease or whether his illness was merely a catalyst. If medical science found a way to cure him, would he return to his old ways? Or was his heart changed forever? How did he really feel about me now? I wanted to talk to somebody, but I was too ashamed and embarrassed to reveal these feelings and questions, fearing that whoever I discussed these matters with would think less of me. I didn't want to reveal my bad feelings to anyone I knew.

I stewed and worried and did nothing for weeks. I wanted to feel better, but I didn't want to do the one task that would help me let go of my grudges: talk to my dad. This wasn't a major offense against the Church, I reasoned, so why involve anyone else? And even if I did talk to him, no doubt he would probably still think less of me even if he tried not to do so.

A short time later I went to the temple. During the ceremony I was impressed with how important harmony with others is, especially in praying to the Lord. I had started to pray for Todd, partially out of guilt and partially because I sincerely wanted him to get better. Was I double-minded in my prayer? Did I say one thing but down deep mean another? I made a resolve to try to work through my resentment toward Todd—for my sake.

On my next trip home, I sat down with my dad to try to talk openly about how I was feeling about Todd. I didn't know if he could understand, but I had to try. I wanted to protect my ego, but simply being in his office almost precluded that. Eventually I was able to tell him everything. Mostly, he listened while I talked, interrupting only occasionally to ask a few questions. He took a deep breath, while blinking back the tears, and started to talk.

"I admire you so much for coming to me and trying to wipe the slate clean with your cousin," he said. Now it was my turn to be surprised! I relaxed. Maybe this would turn out right after all. "I feel impressed that you should tell Todd what you've told me and ask for his forgiveness," he said.

I was bewildered. "I can't do that," I replied. "Do you know how hard it was just to talk to you about this? I just couldn't do that."

"You know that an offense has occurred," he continued, "and because of that, you should go to him and try to resolve the matter. Even though it was years ago, I'm not sure you can get rid of your resentment any other way. You don't have to tell him all of your bad feelings, but you must share some blame for the situation. Taking responsibility is more beneficial for both you and him than discussing details. You can make things worse by giving a lot of explicit details. Instead, avoid justifying yourself and tell him you want to clear up any past concerns about your motives or actions. What matters is that you want to have good feelings between you." Then he read to me from Matthew 5:23–24, which counsels us: "Therefore if thou bring thy gift to the altar, and there rememberest that thy brother hath ought against thee; leave there thy gift before the altar, and go thy way; first be reconciled to thy brother, and then come and offer thy gift."

I stumbled out of his house and somehow made my way home. *It's not right,* I thought. *Todd should apologize to me.* It seemed too hard to go to him after he had wronged me. It would break my heart to go to him and apologize. From somewhere within me, an inner voice repeated a familiar verse: "But blessed are the poor who are pure in heart, whose hearts are broken, and whose spirits are contrite, for they shall see the kingdom of God coming in power and great glory unto their deliverance; for the fatness of the earth shall be theirs" (D&C 56:18).

It took me a long time, but eventually I sat down and wrote a long letter to Todd. I told him that I wanted to get rid of a problem that I had and hoped he would understand why it was easier to write than to call. I tried to put my feelings in positive terms rather than relate all my built-up frustrations over the years. I told him I was praying for both his physical recovery and my own spiritual development.

A few weeks later I got a letter from Todd. It was brief. He said that while some things I said didn't make sense to him, he was glad I had written.

Interesting, I thought. *Maybe he doesn't understand. But so what? I do, and I've shed a heavy burden that has slowed me down for a long time. It's gone, and it feels good to have let it go.*

6

A Believing Heart

I remember clearly the terrible reluctance I had to start praying again. I needed the Lord's help, but I didn't deserve it. I feared that I would find a wall. I wanted a "happy ending" if I decided to pray again, but I knew that it wasn't going to be that easy. I had been away from prayer too long to feel comfortable about praying. Intellectually I believed that the Lord heard and answered prayers. It was possible. But I didn't feel right about it—not now, not after what I had been doing. I believed in repentance too, and forgiveness. I had repented and felt forgiveness in the past. They were possible. It's just that I knew it was necessary to be committed to changing before attempts at prayer or repentance would do any good. And I had a lot of bad habits which I seemed to treasure.

I wasn't out to impress the Lord by faking contrition. Could he accept halfhearted effort for what it was, a feeble attempt to be better? I had always been taught in Primary and Sunday School that the Lord would spew out of his mouth those who were lukewarm. Did that mean me? Could he go more than halfway—say, 90 percent of the way—and nudge me in the right direction? I wouldn't if I were him. But of course I sensed there was a big difference between the two of us. I knew that the Lord knew my delusions, my vain ambitions, and I simply wasn't sure if he was willing to accept me—warts and all—even if I was sure that I was ready to come back.

I was working as the banquet manager of a large restaurant in Houston and really enjoyed what I did. I had worked for several different restaurant chains since my mission and college graduation, and I found this job both satisfying and rewarding. Despite the late hours and frequent Sunday shift obligations, I attended my church meetings enough to teach the Sunday School class for sixteen- and seventeen-year-olds about twice a month.

During the week it was a different story. I was the center of attention among most of the people I worked with. Even though I was only twenty-nine, I was "the old man" among the other employees. I suppose I could have used that position to stop others from drinking and using marijuana, but I didn't. Then after a while I joined in too—at first, just to try it and see what it was like. Although no one had said anything to me, I had always felt like a "prude" for not joining in. I think the sensation of doing something forbidden was more exciting to me than the rush I got from either the alcohol or the pot. Ralph Waldo Emerson was partially right when he said, "If it weren't for taboos, people couldn't enjoy sinning." Although I was married and had two small boys at home, I lived a fancy-free life-style. My view was that since I wasn't hurting anyone and I wasn't sexually promiscuous, what did it matter if I sowed a few wild oats?

Jennifer, of course, rarely complains. Although we have not been married in the temple, she continues to get a temple recommend. She's gone to the bishop for a recommend alone each of the seven years of our marriage.

One night something happened to change my attitude. A party that I had left early was raided by the police. Everyone there was smoking marijuana, of course, and so they were arrested and booked at the local jail. I was lucky. I could have been caught too. I had barely missed the embarrassment and humiliation of calling my wife to get me out of jail.

Suddenly I realized that I wasn't a kid anymore. I wasn't a "big fish in a big pond," I was a doper. Maybe I wasn't a dope addict who needed a fix to avoid withdrawal, but I enjoyed my frequent use of drugs to help me relax, unwind, and have a good time.

Now what? Something had to change. But how could I go to the Lord when the main reason for my remorse was that I almost got caught? How could I pray when I wasn't really sure I was sorry for what I'd done? I had enjoyed myself, had a good time, and made some new friends. Even though I wanted to stop partying the way I had been, my motive for changing was more an interest in staying out of trouble than it was a desire to be good.

Still, I knew what I *should* do even if I wasn't completely committed to doing it. I didn't want to go to a lot of trouble and put forth a major effort to change unless the Lord was going to make it easy on me. And I figured he wouldn't. Why should he? What had I done to deserve any special treatment?

What if nothing happened when I prayed? What if the clarity of prayers that I uttered as a missionary and as a teenager seemed more like a made-up story when I tried again to approach the Lord? Oh, how I wanted to do well with the Lord, to "make it" with him—but without trying too hard! Wouldn't it be nice if there were some prescribed path that I could take and know in advance that it would lead to a desired destination! In my heart I knew there was no map, no certainties that were spelled out for anyone who could read. Rather, there were simply a few guideposts which pointed in a certain direction and left me to figure out the route for myself.

I knew that I had to approach the Lord if I was going to try to change and be better. And there was no time like now to get started. But before I started I decided to read the scriptures suggested in the Topical Guide under the topic "Prayer." In doing so, however, I felt that I was cramming for a final exam without having attended the course. As I read scripture after scripture, I was impressed by what seemed a consistent theme indicating that the Lord is at least as interested in *listening* to our prayers as he is in *answering* them. That is, he wants to know what we think—and how we feel—and he seems to be encouraging us to fully explore our thoughts and feelings with him even if they aren't completely upright and holy. He's heard it all before anyway. He won't be shocked; after all, he knows our hearts. But he wants to hear us say it.

With this in mind I began to pray. As I did I told the Lord I wasn't really certain that I wanted to be "good," just that I wanted to be better than I was. My words seemed so natural and it felt so much as if I were with someone that I kept on praying. I wasn't really looking for an answer, I was simply expressing myself—and being listened to.

Prayer is not to be thought about: it's a matter of doing. There's all the difference in the world between really praying and not really praying. But the experience can't be dissected, taken apart, analyzed, theorized about. Instead, it has to be lived, tasted, known firsthand. It must be experienced. Such praying is simple, requiring that the usual list of requests be put aside for a while. It is not to be taken on with the mentality of success. To pray means to be without guile. In a complex and sophisticated world, it means accepting openness and frankness in a very real conversation with a very dear friend. What could be better?

I didn't want to stop, so I remained kneeling by my bed enjoying the feelings awash within me after I had told the Lord about my faintheartedness and my dilemmas. *Where to from here?* I thought. As these feelings waned, the thought occurred to me that I should go to my bishop and confess my sins.

I quickly sat up. Not that! I didn't think I had done anything that wrong and I certainly didn't want to talk to Bishop Stewart about anything very personal. He was a fine man and all that, but I just didn't relate to him. I suspected he felt the same way about me. "Now, when I was your age . . . ," he would say to me in the church hallway, and then he would go on about something that he had done when he was younger. I knew he meant well, but I didn't feel that he understood me or my problems. But it wasn't only that. I just didn't feel the need to make a confession. I hadn't really done anything that warranted such drastic action.

I fought the feeling for days, then weeks. The more frequently I prayed, the better I felt about myself—and the more vivid the impression that I should go to the bishop and confess. It wasn't that I was overly sensitive about talking to him; it was just that I didn't see the need. It was an impression that I hoped would pass. But it didn't. It stayed with me like an uninvited guest who realizes he has worn out his welcome.

I decided that if I was really going to make a break from my partying life-style I would have to leave behind my friends at the restaurant. So I did the only thing that I could do. I quit my job. Jennifer was elated, even though I didn't have another source of income and no real savings to fall back on. We moved in with a family in the ward who had a couple of spare rooms, and I looked for work and planned my future. Still the feeling wouldn't leave me that I needed to visit with the bishop.

Finally I made an appointment to see him. I would just go and get it over with. As if I were making a trip to the dentist, I would go—on the hunch that it might do some good or at least allow me to get rid of the gnawing feeling I had that I should talk to him.

I made an appointment to see him on a Tuesday night and showed up twenty minutes late, hoping he would have already gone home. He hadn't. He was there waiting for me. I went into his office and he sat across from me with his desk separating us. We carefully picked our way around several topics—the weather, the high school football team, a recent ward dinner. Then he asked me the inevitable: "So why are you here, Mike? How can I help you?"

It hit me the wrong way. *How can you help me?* I thought. *I don't think you can. I don't think I'll give you the pleasure of "helping" me.* Besides, I knew the bishop and his family could use some help themselves. He was so disorganized that ward events seldom went as planned, and his kids were a bunch of smart alecks who never paid attention in my class. *How can you help me?* I thought. *You can't.*

He must have sensed that my silence was not the typical pause that usually goes with collecting one's thoughts. So he tried again. "You . . . I've often thought . . . ," he began. *Here it goes,* I said to myself. "I've often thought that you had great potential to serve in the Church," he said. And so the "patronizing" began. I didn't want to hurt his feelings, but I didn't want to listen to his homespun advice, either.

"Bishop," I interrupted, "I've come to you to confess my sins." The words were out before I could stop them. "I don't know why it's necessary to do it, but I think it's something I must do. I'd like you just to listen, then when I'm through, do whatever you feel is appropriate." Then it all came out, and in more detail than I thought I could remember. When I was through, he looked me in the eye and asked only one question: "Mike, do you believe you have repented of these sins?" I told him that I wasn't sure that I had totally repented, but that I was trying to do so.

Then, unexpectedly, he buried his face in his hands and began to cry. His second oldest son was twenty years old, and the bishop suspected that this son was using drugs. He was disappointed in his son, angry, hurt, upset. He wondered what he could do about it. We talked for a long time, longer than I can ever remember talking to the same person continuously. It was late. I walked behind the desk and did something that is uncharacteristic for me. I put my arm around him.

But before I left his office, he made me make some promises and even write them down. He said that like everyone else, I would have to "walk the talk"; that is, put into action the commitments I had made. I wrote down three things I was going to do and agreed to meet with him four weeks later to report on my commitments.

I left that office changed, converted, determined for the first time in my recollection to keep the commandments of the Lord. I did not then and have not now reached an emotional "promised land." I knew that I had not participated in some kind of man-made self-help scheme but rather had followed the prompting of the Lord and had reaped the benefits of obedience.

The story is told that while hiking once in the mountains with a group of students, Karl G. Maeser pointed to a line of sticks stuck along the edge of a snowbank to mark a trail. The sticks, he emphasized, were like the servants of the Lord. Some were gnarled and withered, others crooked and bent. They were important because of the place they held and the common direction they pointed in.

I left my bishop's office having unexpectedly seen a side of him that I was not prepared for. And I saw a side of myself that I wanted to prepare further. I have never been the same since.

7

When It's Difficult to Say "I'm Sorry"

I guess I first noticed something was wrong when Helen stopped calling me on a regular basis. For the past two years she had called weekly—sometimes just to check in, other times to grumble about something regarding teaching Primary. Frankly, at first I was relieved that she wasn't calling quite so often.

Then I noticed when we worked together on a church project or activity that she was not as friendly with me as I thought our relationship warranted. Almost overnight she had become very short and businesslike whenever she spoke to me. I wasn't sure what was going on. Over a period of several weeks she withdrew from me altogether. Finally a mutual friend said that, without elaborating, Helen had told her I had hurt her feelings badly.

Initially I wondered whether I should go talk to Helen or just let it blow over. Some things can be distorted out of proportion by focusing on them too much and rehearsing supposed grievances. I decided to wait for a little while longer and see what happened. As time passed, however, instead of the situation getting better it got worse. One day at church, Helen and a small cluster of sisters stopped talking when I entered a classroom they were in. I felt very uncomfortable, but I still wasn't sure what was wrong.

I decided to mention the situation to the bishop to see if there was something that had been said to him that would help me determine what I should do. In our conversation I learned that Helen and her husband had also talked to him. They told him that I had acted shabbily, but they didn't say what I had done. I was upset. *Gossips, tattletales!* I thought. I went home angry and sat alone in the dark. What should I do? I recalled the scripture about being offended, the one that taught that whether or not I felt I had caused a problem, if I knew a concern existed I should go to whoever had been offended and try to clear it up. I looked up the specific scripture, Doctrine and Covenants 42:88, hoping I would find some language which might let me off the hook and justify my avoiding speaking directly to Helen. The scripture reads, "If thy brother or sister offend thee, thou shalt take him or her between him or her and thee alone; and if he or she confess thou shalt be reconciled." *Good,* I thought, *if I have offended them they can let me know.*

I had a lingering feeling that I wasn't doing the right thing by just ignoring Helen. I felt bad for days. I needed to do something. But what? I didn't even know what I had done. I certainly couldn't recall doing anything they might find offensive. And to think I had been Helen's confidant for years! It upset me to think they thought I would either intentionally or unintentionally hurt them. I felt we were good enough friends that if there was something I was doing that bothered them, they would tell me about it.

I resisted the impulse to go to them and talk about our estrangement. If I did, maybe they would think I was trying to be "one up" on them by approaching them and admitting that our relationship was less than it had been.

As the months passed and Christmas approached, I resolved that I would not feel better until I went to Helen and talked to her directly. So one night I drove over to Helen's house. I had butterflies in my stomach as I approached her front door. I didn't want to say the wrong thing or be hurt myself. I had never gone to anyone before to try to resolve a difference. I was relieved when Helen's husband opened the door. He was a warm and compassionate man who had recently been released from the bishopric. I knew I could talk to him and he could help me approach Helen in the most effective way possible.

"I would like to talk to you—and to Helen," I said. "Can you help me?"

"I have nothing to say to you and Helen's not feeling well," he replied flatly.

"Could I talk to you for just a few minutes, Richard?" I pleaded.

"I just told you, we have nothing to talk about," he responded. "Good-bye." Then he closed the door.

I was stunned. *Well, I have done my part,* I thought. *They are totally responsible for the situation now.* But then my second thought was that nothing had been resolved. Even though I had come and had done my part, so to speak, nothing had been resolved. I felt I couldn't just go home now.

So I knocked on the door again. I waited patiently, but no one came to the door. *Maybe they didn't hear me,* I thought, so I banged loudly on it. I stood there for a few more minutes and shifted from one foot to the other trying to stay warm and keep my spirits up. I thought, *Well, I am just not going to turn around and go home. I have come too far for that, come to do something important, and I'm not going to leave until I've finished what I came for.*

So I knocked a fourth time. After several minutes Helen came to the door. "I am really sick. I have been in bed all afternoon. The medicine I am taking doesn't seem to be working. Can't you leave me alone?"

"I didn't come to upset you," I replied. "I don't want to take a lot of your time, but I want you to know that I care about you and your family and don't want you to think of me as your enemy. I would never intentionally offend either you or your family, and I want to make amends, if possible, for what I have done that has caused you not to regard me as your friend." I felt vulnerable, open to her comments, hopeful that we could get back on better terms.

"I think you know," she said, as she partially closed the door and peered out from behind its sturdy oaken panels. "You remember, I'm sure," she continued, "that afternoon in September at the church parking lot when I told you that my visiting teachers had not been by for months and that I wanted to call them and tell them such visits were an important duty they were neglecting. Do you remember?"

I did. At the time I did not feel it was appropriate to announce the names of her visiting teachers in front of others who were there in the parking lot. I did not want to embarrass her visiting teachers, who were faithful sisters who could use some encouragement but who would probably resist a reprimand from Helen. I told Helen now that I recalled having said, "It might be better if we talked about this later—privately."

"That's exactly what you said," she replied. "I've never been rebuffed so directly in my life! You would think I was going to gossip about the matter to everyone in the ward. It was plain to see that you didn't trust me! And you never even called or bothered to follow up."

It's true that I had forgotten to get back with her. I told her now that I had unintentionally let the matter slip my mind. I should have followed up. I offered no excuses. I was truly sorry. As I stood on the porch she gradually cracked the door open a little further and then told me about other things she thought I was not handling appropriately as Relief Society president. I listened, asked questions, and showed interest in her suggestions. We stood and talked for a long time.

After about an hour, Richard came by and asked Helen to close the door, since the outside temperatures were dropping rapidly.

"It's getting late," he said to his wife. "You ought to let this intruder leave."

I struggled to keep my composure and control my trembling lip. "I just want you to know that I never intended to offend you and that I am really sorry that I have," I said to Richard.

"I'm glad you finally recognize that," he replied, and he left.

Helen and I soon finished talking, and we said good night to each other. As I got into my car, I was flooded with an overwhelming peace and serenity. I felt so good inside. I wasn't angry and I really wasn't offended by their anger. I was so relieved! Maybe my relationship with Helen wouldn't be as good as it had once been, but at least the turmoil that had existed between us would be dissipated.

In the months since that night on their porch my relationship to both Helen and Richard has gradually improved. They have never brought up that night again nor have they mentioned any of their irritations with my style as Relief Society president. When we have talked, our conversations have been warm and friendly, but they have said nothing about the evening nor have they acknowledged any responsibility for a previously strained relationship. But I don't expect or care about their doing so. Not now. Now I am at peace with myself.

8

A Jump Start from the Lord

Like most people, I have more good days than bad days. There is more joy than sadness, more happiness than heartache, more hope than disappointment in my life. But I struggle. It seems as though I always have. I try to do the right thing at the right time for the right reason. But there are times when seeing what I should do and seeing how I should do it are not always clear. Not that the "big things"—the Word of Wisdom, Sabbath observance, sexual morality—are unclear. Even during those periods in my life when I didn't keep such commandments, I still knew that I should. Guilt can be a powerful tool of the Lord. Rather, when I consider the importance of "little things"—prayer, kindness, charity—I'm convinced there are no "little things."

My life so far has been a series of ups and downs, peaks and valleys, faithful periods followed by selective spiritual amnesia. I'm not certain why I've seemed to play such a silly game of peekaboo with transgression. I would like to say I was "overcome" by sin, but that would give temptation too much credit and provide me with too little blame. To place blame or responsibility on someone else or on circumstances beyond my control would be irresponsible self-deception. My problems are of my own making. Over time I have found solutions to some of them, but doing so has required more than willpower. On my own I would not have been able to make much progress. I needed a jump start from the Lord.

Growing up as a boy in a single-parent inactive LDS home in the forties and fifties provided limited exposure to gospel principles. That is, until my teenage years. Then I encountered seminary. It provided nourishment to a starving soul. For the first time in my life I found something that I was really good at. Spiritually and financially I began to prepare for a mission, yearning for the opportunity to give myself full-time to the service of the Lord.

But when high school was over I had more than a year to wait until I could serve a mission. With no firm direction from anyone I didn't know what to do with my time. So I joined the Marine Corps. I'm still not sure today why I went into the military at that time except that it was common for eighteen-year-olds in the early sixties to join the armed forces. I took this common course without realizing then that it would likely mean I would not serve a mission.

Unfortunately I used my first time away from home to test the limits of acceptable behavior. I wanted to be accepted by my associates and so went along with the crowd rather than maintaining the standards I had been taught in seminary. I knew I wasn't doing what I should, but I didn't have the inner strength to do anything about it. Like Augustine, who wrote in the fifth century A.D., I occasionally prayed, "Lord, make me good —but not yet." I attended church occasionally, and eventually I applied to several universities under the provisions of an "early out" program sponsored by the Marine Corps. Oddly enough, I was accepted only by BYU.

So I went. Trying to make up for lost opportunities, I plunged into available religion classes. When I married in the temple, my wife and I shared common aspirations of celestial marriage and Church service. All seemed right with the world.

After graduating from BYU I attended law school at the University of Utah. During the next three years, as I broadened my academic horizons I narrowed my spiritual perspectives. I became increasingly critical of Church leaders and of what I perceived as the ridiculous ultraconservative political and anti-intellectual hang-ups of people around me. With a change in my peer group, once again I changed too. My wife, on the other hand, became more spiritually enthusiastic; it seemed she was constantly trying to discuss with me the personal discoveries she was making about eternal possibilities. I was embarrassed at her naiveté and tried alternately either to cynically debate with her or to simply ignore her. The result? Both of us became more entrenched in our own positions, she occasionally crying at the end of one of our arguments and I sometimes storming angrily out of the house. Something had to change. We both hoped graduation would make the difference.

I accepted a position with a prestigious law firm in Dallas and began learning the facets of my career in ways law school had only touched upon: negotiating, investigating, and trial procedures. Because local Church membership was sparse and many members were inexperienced, we were immediately placed in administrative positions. Within months I was called as the elders quorum president. I was willing to give Church service a chance as long as people in my ward didn't waste my time.

They did. They bored me. My home teacher would often read faith-promoting stories from Church magazines that I found incredible. "How can you believe that rubbish?" I once asked. "Those stories are to keep children in line, not for adults to believe. You're a well-educated person; how can you repeat that kind of story to another adult?" He stared at me blankly. He did believe it! He told me so! He asked me to pray about such things so that I could know for myself.

I did pray about it. I didn't feel much different. But it seemed to ease some of the tension between my wife and me, so I went along with her for a while and knelt in prayer. But my mind wandered most of the time. It usually wandered back to the office.

I enjoyed my work and the people I worked with. As I relaxed and became comfortable with the office routine during the next couple of years I began to have serious conversations with co-workers and others about intimate matters. I flirted with some of the women I met without giving it a second thought; we were just having a friendly give-and-take conversation. It was all innocent, I thought—not at all like the "serious" discussions I had at home. I didn't try to keep my feelings in check during many of these conversations with others but enjoyed the sensation of being on the edge of something I knew was wrong and then stopping before going too far.

But one night I didn't stop. I went over the brink. And I knew it was wrong. Wrong, in a way, I said to myself, but not all my fault. In fact, after a while I convinced myself that I had simply engaged in a physical act no more right or wrong than eating breakfast or washing my face. So for a time I gave vent to all my natural urgings and I didn't deny myself anything.

It didn't last. It couldn't last. Inside, I had a hounding feeling that I would be "found out." Not that my adultery would be discovered, but that I would be found out as a fraud. Regardless of how hard I tried to blame my wife for not being passionate enough, I knew that I was in the wrong. There was no place to hide; I couldn't escape from me.

After I told her, after I told the high council, after I was excommunicated, I looked for a way to start over and rebuild my life. But my wife said it would have to be without her. It had gone too far.

I never thought it was possible to feel so alone, so homesick with no home to go to. Anywhere. I was lost in the world. It was the same feeling I had had when I was lost once in a large department store as a child. I had frantically run from place to place in the store, looking for a familiar face. I now felt the same way, wishing that I could see a familiar face and run to loving arms and hear reassuring words telling me everything would be all right.

As the weeks and months went by I finally turned to the Lord in frustration. In more a plea than a prayer, I said to him, "I don't know if you exist or not. If you do and if I'm worth the effort, please tell me." I focused all my thoughts, all my emotions, all my energies on that simple request. I kept turning it over and over and over again in my mind, afraid to go to sleep that night and miss an answer. I tossed and turned until I finally fell asleep early in the morning.

When I awoke the next day I went to the mirror and looked at my scraggy reflection. Suddenly I did a double take. Was that me? Had I for an instant seen another reflection? It was as if I had seen a different reflection of *me.* Or had I? I was confused. Something had happened but I couldn't put my finger on what it was. I dismissed it. It wasn't real. *I guess that's what happens with too little sleep,* I thought.

Then another impression. *Read the Joseph Smith story.* I did. I read and reread it several times that day and the next several days. Something had happened to me. I am convinced that I saw in the mirror that morning the person I could become. I could be different. I could change. I *would* do it.

After being out of the Church for more than a year, I was finally rebaptized. It was a glorious day. I had made it back. For the next five years I let worldly distractions—making money, progressing in my firm, gaining social stature—be the main events in my life. And I served again, not only in the elders quorum presidency, but also as a seminary teacher. I was determined to be an example of both gospel scholarship and compassionate service.

As the years passed, I began to forget the turmoil of losing my membership in the Church. After a while, it did seem as though it had happened to someone else and not me. *Good,* I thought, *relief at last from that terrible lonesomeness.*

But it wasn't good. I let myself get involved in a sexual transgression again. No amount of remorse could take away the emptiness and despair I felt. How could I do such a thing? What a despicable bum! I was no better than a vagrant who curled up at night on a park bench with a bottle of cheap wine.

I decided that I simply was no good. I was a telestial person fit for the telestial kingdom only. I needed to admit it, make the most of the situation, and go on. For the next six years, I didn't attend church on Sunday or even think about it much during the week. The only reason I even thought about it six years later was that I remarried and had to answer my wife's questions about my childhood and my past.

We lived comfortably and reasonably contentedly until my teenage son came to live with us. Our world changed. He needed more help and direction than we were prepared to give. So my wife suggested we all go to church together. We felt so natural there that within weeks she was asking for the missionary discussions. Gospel principles and concepts seemed so natural, so logical to her that she was soon ready for baptism.

What about me? What was I ready for? I was ready for the same thing. So I went to my bishop and told him that I wanted to baptize my wife. I also told him that I was ready to put my life in order. I told him *everything*. When I was through, he said that because my transgressions had been so long ago, my confession to him along with my personal commitment to living the gospel principles was sufficient. No formal court would be necessary. That night I gratefully thanked the Lord for a kind and understanding bishop.

My gratitude turned to apprehension when he visited me a few days later and said he had made a mistake. After conferring with the stake president, it was determined that a court would be necessary. Scenes from my life came parading back to my recollection in a kind of slow motion single file. I couldn't move. I couldn't possibly imagine anything more humiliating than going back to a high council court and admitting that it wasn't the first time that I had been there. I told him I needed some time to think.

I did think about it. But I was reluctant to do it. How could I ask for a second chance? Was it worth doing all this for Denise? Was I that committed to it? Was I willing to go through it all? And could I follow through and avoid temptations in the future if I was forgiven? I wondered.

While weighing all of these questions and evaluating my options I came upon a scripture in a family home evening lesson I was preparing. I read it again and again. I sat immovable in my chair thinking about its implications. My arms and legs felt so heavy that I literally could not move them. The passage states:

> Nevertheless, notwithstanding the great goodness of the Lord, in showing me his great and marvelous works, my heart exclaimeth: O wretched man that I am! Yea, my heart sorroweth because of my flesh; my soul grieveth because of mine iniquities.
>
> I am encompassed about, because of the temptations and the sins which do so easily beset me.
>
> And when I desire to rejoice, my heart groaneth because of my sins; nevertheless, I know in whom I have trusted. (2 Nephi 4:17–19.)

So even prophets have problems! *But not the kind of problems I have,* I protested. Then for some reason I don't fully understand I remembered a story related by a returned missionary in our elders quorum discussion years ago. He said that while in the old missionary home in Salt Lake City, President Joseph Fielding Smith, then the President of the Quorum of the Twelve, had spoken to the missionaries about avoiding circumstances which place them beyond their ability to resist temptation. He reportedly told the missionaries that if he allowed himself to be in the wrong place at the wrong time, he could fall victim to sin and immorality. He explained that anyone can fall and that he was not exempt, and that no one ever reaches a condition of being safe from transgression.

That was all I needed. I went to the court. I was embarrassed and humiliated to admit that this was not my first appearance before such a court. I searched their faces for signs of cynicism or jeers or indications that they thought I was simply an unrepentant sinner, but found nothing on their faces but compassion. I breathed a sigh of relief, knowing that as difficult as it would be to come back to the Church, I would have the help of others and not their resentment.

I was again excommunicated. I knew that would happen. But I believed the stake president when he assured me that through sincere and thorough repentance I could once again enjoy full fellowship in the Church.

It was easy to believe him then as I was beginning the long, hard road back. But as time passed and no apparent efforts were made for me to be rebaptized, I became discouraged. Maybe I was wrong about the faces of compassion at the high council meeting. Maybe they thought I was just an old reprobate who was not worth saving. I wanted to shout down my self-doubts, but they were more piercing than they were loud, and not so easily dismissed. In anguish I turned to the Lord: "I am only human. How can I overcome this? It's too much for me. Please, please help me." And though I was in desperation, I was not left alone. In individual and personal ways the Lord buoyed me up and offered companionship in quiet moments of self-critical analysis.

Eventually I was rebaptized and two years later I met with a General Authority to have my priesthood blessings restored. After a searching interview he made a remarkable statement to me. He said that it was likely that our paths would cross again in the future and that he would realize that we had met but would not remember where it was or any of the circumstances of our meeting. He said it was the Lord's way of demonstrating that forgiveness was complete.

My own memory fades regarding those events as time passes. They seem more like a bad movie that I wish I had never seen than a part of my own past. However, when I counsel youth in my calling as a member of the bishopric, I am sensitive to just how vulnerable we all are. Brigham Young tried to illustrate that when Thomas B. Marsh, who was excommunicated when he was President of the Quorum of the Twelve Apostles, asked to be rebaptized almost nineteen years later. After an interview with President Young, Brother Marsh asked to speak to the assembled Saints at the old Bowery on Temple Square. In asking for the forgiveness of the Saints and to demonstrate that his repentance was complete, he promised that if he was accepted back into the congregation by the Saints, he would never falter again in doing his duty.

Brigham Young then arose to speak. He commented that when Brother Marsh and others were chosen to be members of the Quorum of the Twelve, "I looked upon them as men of great powers of mind—as men of ability—men who understood the things of heaven." However, he added that Brother Marsh had not learned a thing in being out of the Church some nineteen years.

> If he had good sense and judgment, he would not have spoken as he has. He has just said, "I will be faithful, and I will be true to you." . . . He has told me that he would be faithful, and that he

> would do this and the other; but he [doesn't] know what he will do next week or next year.
>
> I do not know what I shall do next year; I always speak for the present. . . . You never heard me say that I was going to be true to my God; for I know too much of human weakness: but I pray God to preserve me from falling away—to preserve me in the truth. I depend not upon myself; for I know too much of human weakness and of myself, to indulge in such remarks. (*Journal of Discourses*, 5:212–13.)

I realize, more than most people perhaps, that in this life it is never too late to repent and that it is never possible to be beyond temptation's influence.

9

Sins of Omission

"Hi, honey," My husband's voice rang out on the other end of the telephone. "I may be a little late in coming home from work. Do you have any plans for tonight?"

"Yes, it's homemaking meeting tonight. It's always on the third Wednesday of the month. Did you forget?" I asked.

"Okay. No problem. I can still make it before you leave, I think. What time does it start?"

"Seven," I said. "But I don't want to be late. I need to leave by six to help some of the teachers set up." I tried to have enough urgency in my voice to make sure he knew I meant it.

"I'll make it. Gee, it's great to be married to the ward Relief Society president," he said without a hint of sarcasm in his voice. "Lots of benefits. Look, for instance, at all the time I get to spend alone with the kids. Will you be able to make dinner before you leave?"

"Probably not," I responded. "Look at it as being another benefit. You get to practice your cooking skills. There's pizza in the freezer."

I had always been a very organized person who liked having everything in its place. But lately it just didn't seem that there was time to do the things which *had* to be done, let alone the things I simply wanted to do. With five children ranging from three to thirteen, there was always someone who needed to be taken somewhere for some activity or other—piano, soccer, Scouts, dance. Our BMW (Big Mormon Wagon) hardly ever stopped to rest. Being called as the Relief Society president demanded that we carefully coordinate our schedules so that everyone arrived at the right place at the right time.

Time—there never seemed to be enough of it. As I hurried off to homemaking meeting I regretfully noted all the things that were still undone: dirty dishes in the sink, dirty clothes in the laundry basket, dirty faces on my children. Cleanliness may be next to godliness, but it was also next to impossible.

The homemaking meeting went well. As we finished cleaning up, the bishop called and asked if I would wait for him. When he arrived he informed me that Bob Dailey was out of work again. He asked me to make an appointment and complete an order for the bishops' storehouse.

Oh, great! I thought. *The Daileys are back on Church welfare again! He isn't even a member of the Church, and his wife only comes to church when it's convenient for her to attend. He's so undependable that he can't keep a job for longer than a few months. They're just taking advantage of the Church and playing on the bishop's sympathy. It's too bad! The bishop has such a hard time turning people like that down.* But I didn't voice any of my concerns. I knew the bishop would tell me that we shouldn't judge others and that we would only help the Daileys for a few weeks. We had talked about the Daileys before, during their previous periods of unemployment. And if the bishop was anything, he was predictable.

I called and went by the Daileys' place the next day. They lived in a trailer off a dirt road that was hard to get to when it rained, as it had that morning. When I arrived Sister Dailey handed me a long list of food and commodities that she wanted. I bit my tongue and took a deep breath, then explained why some items needed to be eliminated or reduced or changed.

While I was doing this, Bob's only movement was to reach for the remote control instrument and switch the television channels. For her part, Sister Dailey would interrupt me occasionally and tell her husband to turn to a certain program. As I looked around the trailer I was aghast. There were empty cans and bottles on every table and chair within sight. Candy wrappers were scattered on the floor, and a cat and her litter of kittens were using a litter box in another corner. Eventually I got through my explanation and left the trailer.

"Bishop," I said when I got him on the phone, "I've been to the Daileys and have their order for you to sign. But I want you to know that I don't feel good about this. I think they're just using us."

"Things didn't go well?" he asked in his usual reflective-listening mode.

"Oh, there were no particular problems," I said. "It's just that they seem to be doing so little to help themselves. Their place is a mess, and Brother Dailey was simply lounging around all the time I was there. He is not helpless. At least he could give his wife a hand around the house."

"Maybe I'd better talk to them," he said. "We could discuss some job-finding techniques to get him back to work again."

"Good idea. And tell him to help his wife clean the house."

I didn't hear back from the bishop again until later in the week.

"Sister Dailey just called. She said there was a complaint made about them to the Public Health Service, and a warning was issued after the officials came out to their place," he said.

"I'm not surprised," I heard myself say.

"She's pretty upset and worried," he continued. "They threatened to take her children to the Methodist group home over on Third Street if things didn't improve. Could you get several sisters together and go over and help her? I'm going to ask the priesthood to help in the yard. I feel that if we can help them get back on their feet things will go better."

"I'll try, Bishop, but it won't be easy," I said. "I think the Daileys have complained about so many things not to their liking in the ward that it may be hard to get very many sisters to go—and I don't blame them. But I'll do the best I can."

My compassionate service leader and I were able to get four sisters to go over to the Daileys' trailer and clean up on that Friday. Brother Dailey wasn't there because he had some job leads to check on, Sister Dailey said. *I'll bet,* I said to myself.

We spent the afternoon cleaning and scrubbing and left some copies of pamphlets on housekeeping tips. Tired and resentful, I went home to my own household chores. I felt used.

That Sunday the bishop called me into his office.

"I'm so grateful for the things you do for people in the ward," he said. "I know you do many things which I do not see, some of them at considerable personal sacrifice. You are a willing and dependable worker."

"Why all of a sudden are you giving me these compliments?" I asked suspiciously.

"You know me too well," he laughed. "Or am I that transparent? Or are you that perceptive? Regardless, I think the Lord is pleased with the service you render. I would like you to talk in sacrament meeting in five weeks on the topic 'Why Do We Serve One Another?' Will you do that?"

"Of course," I replied. "But is there some reason you're telling me so far in advance?"

"Yes, there is," he responded. "I'd like you to read everything you can on the subject in the scriptures and in the *Ensign* for the next two weeks. Then you'll have a month left to see if any of these new discoveries make a difference in your life, and you can report to us on them in sacrament meeting. Sister Davis, some people are gifted with innately compassionate hearts. But most of us must consciously seek to develop compassionate personalities. I don't think there is any magical formula that says how to develop this talent. Like any other personal attribute, it takes hard work, difficult decisions, hanging on, trying again, and not giving up."

I spent the next two weeks reading as I had been requested to do. Since I was reading with such a single-minded focus, it seemed that each new article or scriptural reference brought renewed personal insights. I recorded my discoveries in my journal and wrote what they meant to me. Over and over, I discovered in my reading that it seemed the Lord was not only interested in *how* we served but also in *why*—the purpose or reason for our service. Service was a matter of the heart and much more than a handout. As the Apostle Paul wrote: "But this I say, He which soweth sparingly shall reap also sparingly; and he which soweth bountifully shall reap also bountifully. Every man according as he purposeth in his heart, so let him give; not grudgingly, or of necessity: for God loveth a cheerful giver." (2 Corinthians 9:6–7.) And again, "Though I bestow all my goods to feed the poor . . . and have not charity, it profiteth me nothing" (1 Corinthians 13:3).

I thought about the moral superiority I had felt toward some of the welfare recipients of the past year. Some were truly needy, I had decided earlier, while others were not. Now, as I reflected on it, I kept coming back to a single thought. Maybe those who didn't appreciate my acts of service or who were on a spiritual dole system were the real measure of my compassion. Maybe they were the only measure. This did not mean waiting hand-and-foot on others who could or should do for themselves. It simply seemed to mean that acts of service should not be done begrudgingly or out of duty or for any other reason than being motivated by the pure love of Christ.

Easier said than done, I thought. But the more I read in the *Ensign* about Latter-day Saints who had served others unselfishly, the more I wanted to purify my own heart. Then in the Book of Mormon I read this passage about charity: "Wherefore, my beloved brethren, pray unto the Father with all the energy of heart, that ye may be filled with this love, which he hath bestowed upon all who are true followers of his Son, Jesus Christ" (Moroni 7:48).

So I prayed, "Heavenly Father, help me to believe that thou canst change my heart. Help me to believe that this is possible."

As I prayed, all of a sudden I realized why I begrudged helping some people. They had disrupted my schedule badly and I wanted an apology from them! I wanted an absolute apology for the inconveniences and missed soccer practices and late charges for overdue bills and all the other things I didn't get done because I was helping them. I wanted an acknowledgment of all of the hassles and problems and misfortunes I went through on their behalf. I had no doubt that this was my just due. It was only fair.

Sitting there, I recognized that I was expecting something which never would happen, never could happen. I realized then that I was burdening myself with the wrong concerns. Instead of worrying about what was fair I needed to focus on what Jesus would do. He was not seeking others' gratitude at every turn. He healed ten lepers and didn't resent the fact that only one returned to give him thanks.

I tried for the next thirty days to apply these principles in my daily life. By admitting to myself that I had been resentful of the inconveniences of and others' ingratitude toward my service, I was freed from this resentment's hold on me. Confession can do that.

During the next few weeks I felt more contented with my life than I had ever felt before. I noticed more ways to show kind, tender concern for others than I had before. My family in particular noticed this change, and quarreling over chores and household tasks diminished. Even Sister Dailey called me on the phone just to talk! She needed a friend and suddenly felt that I could be her confidant. For my part, I no longer considered such acts of kindness as "service." There was no credit expected.

I don't remember all of the things I said at that sacrament meeting. It was more difficult to convey how I had changed than I thought it would be. Like an artist who can merely duplicate the facade of a building and not its history or context, I could only relate events. I felt something was lost in the translation for most of the congregation. As I finished, I turned to look at the bishop and saw by his radiant, glowing face that he understood. Somehow, I think he knew all along.

10

A Long and Difficult Road

I guess I have always known there were other people in the Church who have problems, but none of them seem to be like mine. Somehow, other people's lives always seem to be so "right," so all-together. I'm not idolizing anyone; it's just that my problems are so different. It's difficult to think of the finer points of perfection when the ordinary problems that I struggle with would be as remote to most of my ward members as a visit to a Third World country. This makes me reluctant to talk about my problems. But in the telling there is hope—hope that I can develop a better sense of who I am and thereby gain a perspective on what I can become.

My father and two of my brothers are ministers in the Baptist church. My sister and one other brother are Baptist believers although they are not active church members. My remaining brother is a Latter-day Saint, but inactive. My husband's folks are also Baptists. I became a member of the Church in 1967. I had been married to Keith for six months and he was serving in the United States Navy in Japan. I didn't have Keith's permission to be baptized (an oversight on the part of the missionaries and the man who was then our branch president), but I didn't think my husband would mind.

But Keith reacted with unexpected anger, as did my folks and his, to the news of my baptism. I felt that when he got home and we were physically close again, his attitude would change. I was mistaken. He not only refused to hear the good news of the restored gospel but he also refused to allow me to be active in the Church.

I recall the struggle I had during those early years. I never was able to seriously consider divorce; I thought my faith and prayers would win Keith over, and I loved him so much that I couldn't imagine any future without him. Loving the two sons I've borne as I do, whenever I've considered separating them from their father, I weigh the results and realize that none of us would truly benefit. Keith would certainly never consider investigating a church that breaks up families. The boys may resent the Church for being the cause of depriving them of their father. I felt that even I could not be happy "alone"; being with a good person I love seemed to be better than being alone.

So to keep peace in our home and to save my new marriage I became physically inactive in the Church. But I always knew it was true and longed to be there in person, not just in spirit.

For a time, I practiced the old adage "go along to get along" in experimenting in some group sex-related activities with Keith—activities that I knew were wrong—until I could indulge my husband no longer. I knew some of the things we were doing were wrong even though he said that the Bible teaches that "wives [should] submit yourselves unto your own husbands" (Ephesians 5:22). No amount of self-justification could get me through such things. So I faced a kind and sympathetic branch president and sobbed my confession that I had participated with my husband in infidelity. How embarrassed and ashamed I was to have to recall and tell him some of the incidents. But I think my fear of excommunication was stronger than any other feelings I faced at that time, for I knew for certain that Keith would never agree to let me be rebaptized. The branch president held a Church court, and I fasted and prayed not only for forgiveness from the Lord and the Church, but mostly that I wouldn't forever lose my membership. But through it all, I felt that I was unworthy, weak, too fearful, too unreliable to ever be fit for the kingdom of God. The court decided that I could retain my membership—perhaps more because of my forced inactivity than their belief that I could ever be a truly productive member. However, I was grateful for the blessing of remaining in the Church, though still inactive, and I began studying the scriptures and Church publications and doing genealogy work.

My husband never knew of my interviews with the branch president, but when I refused to participate in any more "games," our relationship gradually changed. We remained husband and wife but were no longer friends. We have been married for almost twenty years now, and except for our occasional nighttime closeness, we are but polite strangers. Keith has been through college, has taught for twelve years, and is finishing a course this spring to become an elementary school principal. He has grown academically while I have grown spiritually.

Unfortunately, Keith is no closer now to listening to the gospel than he was nineteen years ago.

Last year I decided to begin going to sacrament meetings. The two Sundays I went, I returned to an empty house. I spent the remainder of those two Sundays in tears, worrying and searching the countryside for my family. They arrived home later in the evening both times. Keith refused to speak to me for more than a month. I fasted and prayed to know what to do. A couple of months later I was reading Elder James E. Talmage's book *The Articles of Faith* and this answer came to me: "Wives also, even though their husbands be not of their faith, are not to vaunt themselves and defy authority, but to be submissive, and to rely upon gentler and more effective means of influencing those whose name they bear" (James E. Talmage, *The Articles of Faith* [Salt Lake City: The Church of Jesus Christ of Latter-day Saints, 1966], p. 420).

From the time I discovered that, I have felt less burdened by my forced inactivity. I have decided to be more of a good example of Church membership. I have also decided to teach my children the gospel as best I can at home, whatever the repercussions; and most important, I have decided to stop hiding my Church books. When they get knocked off the tables, I just pick them up again. I have decided to bear my testimony often to anyone who will listen. I have decided to stop avoiding discussions with my family and instead to listen to their discussions of Bible scriptures and to comment when I can. I have decided to *be* a Mormon! Would you believe that I'm a different person? Now I say, "I don't have what I really want, but I am going to do the best I can with what I have." And I have learned to live one day at a time and to take each problem one at a time. I haven't seen any change in my husband's beliefs, but now at least we discuss the household budget. My dad and brothers are still preaching fire and brimstone, but my dad has told my sister that he believes I'll go to heaven! I haven't been to sacrament meeting this year and only attended three times last year, but I have a lovely friend whose husband isn't a member either, and we encourage each other. Since she's able to be active in the Church, she brings me programs from sacrament meetings and has even taped some Sunday School and Relief Society meetings for me. She also got me involved in the LDS Book Club and the Pursuit of Excellence program; and even got me "called" as her companion in Relief Society visiting teaching. (I sometimes feel guilty and uncertain whether I am doing right by doing this without Keith's consent or knowledge.)

I'm still fasting and praying for things to change with Keith. My patriarchal blessing says I should be prepared to go to the temple "when" my husband accepts the gospel. But now I fast and pray with a different attitude than I had years ago, for I realize that Heavenly Father, though he loves me as much as he loves anyone else, will not interfere with Keith's free agency. It's up to me to set the example and the Church reading material before him as much as possible, but I must allow him to choose, just as I did.

So many times I've felt as if my prayers have hit a brick wall and bounced back. I've wondered where my Heavenly Father was. Was he too busy to hear my feeble cries for help and understanding? For years my prayers, though faithfully "said" morning and evening, were stilted, repetitive, and boring even to me, so I wondered how Father, who knows all things, could possibly be interested in hearing my broken record. I have sometimes tried very hard to imagine myself in the presence of the Lord. What would I say? Would I be nervous? How familiar or formal should I be? As I've tried to drop my defenses and not worry about protocol, but instead imagine him in real but ordinary surroundings, I've changed. I remember that once as I knelt to pray, I said simply, "Dearest Father, I love thee, I need thee. Help me to know thee as my Father." When I have felt as if I were projecting myself into his presence, he has seemed less like a stranger and more like a relative I haven't seen in a while and have decided to call.

My husband isn't a mean and stubborn person. He is proud and self-reliant and something of a skeptic. But he's also good to the children and to his family. He's dependable. He's kind to those in need. His students and colleagues adore him. Without really knowing it, he keeps the Word of Wisdom. When we first met I smoked and drank coffee and tea. Keith never did those things. He doesn't overindulge in anything. He's made mistakes—and we've made some together. But I disappointed him. We were both raised in Baptist homes. Smoking, coffee, and tea were okay, but dancing, music in the church, even Sunday School were not okay. Neither was it okay for women to wear makeup, dress in pants, or cut their hair. I left my parents' teaching, joined the Church, and began to do all those things. When I became a Mormon, I became a sinner in their eyes. Our brief encounter with adultery was not all his doing. I so much wanted him to love me that I nearly let myself be led "carefully down to hell." When I realized where I was, I knew inwardly that Keith was probably testing my sincerity in the Church, and that bothered me as much as the long road of repentance that I was facing. But I always knew that if I'd protested from the beginning, it never would have gone that far—because Keith is so basically good and strong.

Some people don't change easily. And of course some don't change at all regardless of how much others love them, teach them, accept them. In the end choosing our own road is what life is all about. As much as I would like things to be different, they aren't. And they may not change much, either. But I am able to choose for myself the kind of person I'll be too. Maybe not completely in the way that those who talk about "positive mental attitude" describe it, because I do care what others think. In a very real way, I believe we are what we think other people think we are. I can allow myself to be influenced by those who already think I have the innate ability to become a child of God in every sense of the word. I can become as he is.

Platitudes are nice, a friend used to say, but they don't plant corn or harvest wheat. Still there is something to be said about ideas changing the world. Or a person. As I've changed I've been less troubled about whether Keith changes or not. I want him to change, but in the same way I'd like the world to change. I'm no longer ashamed nor do I pity myself for I see more clearly now than before that I must simply do my best.

I think I've learned a lot about changing myself and not demanding changes in others as I've watched different people care for children who are not their own. There is an elderly couple whose own rebellious son disappointed them and married a woman they did not approve of. But because they loved their son, they welcomed his wife and her teenage child from a previous marriage into their home and hearts. Within two years the marriage ended in divorce. The teenage boy was once again adrift, alone, lonely. Then this elderly couple stepped forward. They wanted this boy to stay with them. They loved him. It didn't matter whose child the boy was legally. As far as they were concerned, he was "theirs." They didn't want anything from him or expect him to grow up in a certain way, although they did read to him from the scriptures. Sometimes he goes to church with them and sometimes he doesn't.

Perhaps when my husband sees me sharing others' burdens in the same way as that elderly couple—through the restored gospel—he will finally understand that I care for him with no strings attached.

11

As He Thinketh in His Heart

I awoke with a start. What was I going to do about that recurring dream? I didn't want it, but there it was. Again. Why couldn't I make it go away? I got up to get a drink of water and sit on the couch in the living room. At least if I stayed awake I wouldn't have the same dream again. Besides, it just felt good to be awake and to listen to Cheryl and the kids as they slept. It was a reassuring feeling that seemed to say everything was all right. Even if it wasn't.

As a member of the bishopric I had often counseled the youth in our ward to think good, clean thoughts and had promised them that if they would the Lord would bless them for it. In the teachers quorum when we had talked about avoiding R-rated movies, I had told them that by doing so, they would not need to worry about undesirable "flashbacks"—lewd, graphic scenes that would race through their minds without conscious recall—or about unnecessary memories. Now I sat here with a scene that kept coming to me as I slept; and my conscience seemed to say, "You hypocrite! How can you teach the youth of the ward about morality when you have such dreams?"

It all started at the beginning of the school year. I teach math at the local high school. A young woman—Karen Taylor—had just graduated and accepted her first teaching assignment at our school. She taught Spanish, and since the principal knew I had served a mission to Mexico he asked if I would befriend her. As the only LDS teacher at the school, I would have considered it my missionary obligation to do so even if he had not asked.

As we became acquainted and the weeks and then months went by, I saw what a sincere and genuine person Karen was. She came to dinner several times at our home, listened to three missionary lessons, and attended church once. But she didn't read the Book of Mormon or pray much. She decided that she wasn't ready to be committed to any church just then and hoped that I would understand. She also said she hoped I would still be her friend. I reassured her that I would, of course, and made an extra effort to go by her room, comment on bulletin board displays, see her at school dances, and talk to her at the faculty lounge. She in turn responded by baking a birthday cake for me, helping with National Honor Society activities that I was the faculty advisor to, and volunteering to run errands for me occasionally.

But I had a problem. I was attracted to her. In my recurring dream, I would meet Karen at the top of an isolated, windswept hill, run hand-in-hand in slow motion with her to a grassy knoll, embrace—and then I would wake up. I was so ashamed of myself, so embarrassed. I wanted to hide. Why had a simple friendship turned into something else? How could I let myself do this? I wanted to get rid of these unwanted feelings—to replace them with good, positive, wholesome ones. But it seemed that the harder I tried, the more they stayed with me. By concentrating on the feelings and trying to discard them, I became more aware during my waking hours of them. Sometimes even during my silent personal prayer my mind would wander and this dream would vividly come to me. Disgusted with myself, I would close my prayer and sit on the edge of the bed. I felt I was living a lie.

I needed help. But where could I go? I wanted to talk to Cheryl about this, tell her everything; but I couldn't. How could I tell my wife that I had inappropriate dreams about someone else? I was afraid that she would think less of me. Even though she might understand, I didn't want to take the chance. Cheryl was proud of me—proud of me as a loving husband, a caring father, and a worthy priesthood bearer. I valued greatly the look in her eyes when I conducted sacrament meeting, gave an award to one of the youth, or reported to her on a leadership meeting. I didn't want to lose any of that. And what about the bishop? He was so busy; he didn't need to be burdened by the problem of one of his counselors. And what would he think? Would he not want to trust me in the future if I told him? Would he think that I had a "roving eye" and wonder each time he saw me with a sister in the ward what I was really up to? I didn't want to talk to him. I couldn't chance it. Besides, I hadn't *done* anything wrong. I didn't see that I had to confess to him. Maybe I could work it out on my own.

But "affairs of the heart" are not easily dismissed. Even though I went out of my way to avoid Karen at school, it still seemed that we often ended up at the same place at the same time—on bus duty, in the faculty lounge, in the parking lot—and often there was no one else around. I found myself noticing little details about her—the curl of her eyelashes, a tiny mole on her right cheek, the way she carried her books—and I often literally had to jerk my head to one side and focus my attention on a nearby object to think of something else.

What was I going to do? The more I tried to avoid debasing thoughts, the more I became aware of them. The harder I tried, the less successful I seemed to be. I was even becoming more critical of Cheryl at home—the way she kept the house, things she did with the kids, meals that weren't prepared when I was ready to eat. When she would ask what was wrong, I would pass off my irritability as simply tension due to projects at school or papers that needed grading or some other excuse. It was apparent that she recognized something was wrong, but she obviously didn't know what it was. Oh, how I wished I could tell her! Instead, I hugged her and tried to reassure her that nothing was really wrong —even though there was something very wrong.

I was very aware of passages of scripture which indicated that our negative thoughts would condemn us as much as our negative acts. And I remembered that the Savior had said that if a man looked on a woman to lust after her, he had committed adultery already in his heart. But I didn't think I had lust in my heart. Or did I? Frankly, I wasn't sure just exactly what was and what wasn't lust.

I didn't want to minimize or rationalize what I was going through. But I didn't want to make it a bigger deal than it was, either. I had always considered lust as similar to seduction. While I knew that I was not pursuing anyone or even flirting, I *had* given in to some unwholesome feelings. I had removed some of my attention from my wife and directed it to another. Although no sexual act had occurred or even been contemplated, my feelings were unfaithful and untrue to my wife. And my wife was intuitively aware that something was wrong. She had detected that I was withholding something from her. Our relationship was frayed because my unconditional allegiance to her was being swayed.

Since I didn't feel that I could talk to Cheryl or that I needed to talk to the bishop, and since I wasn't effective in talking to the Lord about this problem, I turned to an old friend—the scriptures. Surely if I searched long enough I would find not merely condemnation but guidance. And I did. In Alma 39:9–10, I found these verses: "Now my son, I would that ye should repent and forsake your sins, and go no more after the lusts of your eyes, but cross yourself in all these things; for except ye do this ye can in nowise inherit the kingdom of God. Oh, remember, and take it upon you, and cross yourself in these things. And I command you to take it upon you to counsel with your elder brothers in your undertakings."

These verses both reminded me of my need to redirect my thoughts and feelings and showed me that such inclinations were a cross that I could bear by talking about such a problem openly with my "elder brothers." Fortunately I do have an older brother who knows me in ways that no one else knows me, who doesn't worry about telling me just exactly what he thinks, and with whom I would be safe in revealing that I wasn't perfect. He already knows I am not perfect. In fact, he can detect pretension at a considerable distance. And since he was a bishop himself in another city, I knew his advice would be realistic and positive.

I made arrangements to meet with him after work so that we would be able to spend some time alone. After all the usual preliminaries, I got to the point. He was neither shocked nor surprised. As we talked, he suggested that perhaps I was trying so hard to dismiss my unwanted thoughts and feelings that my concentrated focus on those feelings served instead to keep them before me. "You can't try hard to forget something," he said. "Instead you must replace such thoughts or feelings with something stronger and more direct." He read another scripture to me from Christ's teachings to the Nephites:

> Behold, it is written by them of old time, that thou shalt not commit adultery;
>
> But I say unto you, that whosoever looketh on a woman, to lust after her, hath committed adultery already in his heart.
>
> Behold, I give unto you a commandment, that ye suffer none of these things to enter into your heart;
>
> For it is better that ye should deny yourselves of these things, wherein ye will take up your cross, than that ye should be cast into hell. (3 Nephi 12:27–30.)

In our conversation my brother and I decided that when unwanted thoughts or feelings come, they must be denied; that is, not given access, refused a place. If they linger outside, waiting for a chance to come in, we must concentrate on something else. Without scrutiny, examination, and close inspection any feeling will wither away. The importance of attention cannot be underestimated. So rather than our trying to "force" unwanted feelings out through sheer willpower—which sometimes cannot be done—we should replace those feelings through intense concentration on something else. To love the scriptures, or to admire a piece of music, or to cling to a righteous life, we need to give it our attention. We need to "gaze" on it, not once but again and again, to return to it in different moods for different reasons.

I went home buoyed and uplifted. I started focusing on the little details in my family's everyday life that I enjoyed. For the first time since I was a missionary, I began writing in my journal, trying very hard to record in detail how five-year-old Kevin played with three-year-old Rachel. I also wrote about particular kids at school—habits that annoyed me and pranks that amused me. Church meetings, too, became an opportunity to notice the interaction of ward members in detail. I tried with renewed emphasis to practice what I preached: in addition to the tried and true practices of regular attendance at meetings, fasting, prayer, and scripture reading, I worked at more difficult matters such as compassionate giving, patience, and understanding.

When I felt that I was acting hypocritically, I did not stop trying to live well. I kept trying. I turned my attention to things which really mattered and found an inner strength and desire for doing good that I didn't realize I had. And I am better for it. My capacity to worship the Lord and do his will has increased and deepened.

12

How Could They Ask for So Much?

I could not believe what I was hearing. I was shocked and more than a little annoyed.

"You want me to contribute *how* much to the ward budget?" I asked with some irritation in my voice.

The bishop's counselor, Bob Thomas, repeated the amount again. It was considerably more than I expected to contribute. It was almost twice as much as I had contributed the year before. The reasons for the request were not new to me. Nonetheless, they were recited by Brother Thomas once again for my benefit: depressed economic conditions had forced several families to relocate elsewhere while others had been indefinitely laid off by a large manufacturing company in the city. As the high councilor responsible for employment in the stake, I didn't really need such a reminder. I especially didn't need it from Bob Thomas. Bob and I had graduated from high school together years ago and eventually were employed in the same division of a large food processing company. Bob was a thin man, the kind who gets lost in a shirt. He was in accounting and had only been promoted once in eleven years of employment. By contrast, I was the youngest section head in our division. People around me often said that I was on the "fast track." So when Bob was called into the bishopric, I was always a little anxious about giving him my tithing slip and knowing that he knew just how much my salary was.

Now I wondered if he was using it against me. It was not that I couldn't contribute as much as I was being asked to give. I could, but it would be hard to do. We would have to cut out some things that we had planned to do that year—including, perhaps, two trips to the temple in Atlanta with overnight stays. We would have to alter plans that I didn't want to change.

So this is it, I thought as I stared blankly back at Bob. *This is how you're going to get back at me. This is how you're going to handle your own career disappointments and frustrations—by trying to deny me some of the extras I've earned. Petty, Bob, very petty,* I thought.

"It's a little steep, isn't it?" was all I managed to say.

"I know it will be a sacrifice," Bob responded, "but the Lord has asked us to sacrifice to build up this kingdom. . . ."

Bob continued talking but my thoughts were elsewhere. The message was one that I had heard before, that I had even spoken before. It was not that I wasn't willing to sacrifice; I was. If I was convinced that the Lord really wanted me to contribute that much, I would do so. I just wasn't convinced. Instead, I figured Bob, not the Lord, was testing me. I was backed into a corner.

"I'll think about it," I responded when he was finished talking. "I need to discuss the amount we can contribute as a family and I'll get back to you."

I did talk to my wife. When we were alone and I explained the request, she slumped down in a chair with anguish written in her face.

"It's not fair. There are so many things we need," she said. And she began to name them: braces for Ryan's teeth, surgery for Russell's extra molars, new glasses for Kristen, special shoes for Kirk, piano and saxophone lessons, and on and on.

Neither one of us felt good about the request. But we wanted to do the right thing. We decided to think about it and pray about it for a week.

But the more I prayed the worse I felt—not about the amount I was being asked to give but about the request itself. I didn't deserve to be treated like this. I didn't deserve such a predicament. I gave lots of time and energy and even money to the Church. In my Church calling and in personal ways, I tried to do the right thing.

I'll bet no one else is being asked to give this much, I said to myself. *I'm just an easy target. I can make up the difference for several other families so they're really loading me up. Probably no one else is being asked to give this much, even on a percentage basis. They think I'm a moneybags just because I've got a good job. Well, I've earned it. I've worked hard for what I have. No one gave it to me on a silver platter. Even now, I'm still at work long after most peple have gotten home, eaten their dinner, and played with their kids.*

I brooded over my dilemma into the next week, avoiding Bob at church that Sunday. *Is this the chink in my spiritual armor?* I wondered. *Is this what it comes down to—that I'll give of my time, talents, and possessions—all that I have been blessed with—but only up to a point? I'll go so far, but no further, is that it?* "Aha, you are already lost!" It was a familiar voice, a voice within me. If I contributed grudgingly, what virtue would there be in that? If I gave a lesser amount than was requested, how could I show that I sustained my local leaders? I was caught in a trap I had devised myself. I didn't have to make it a big issue—it could have been a simple matter of agreeing to the request or to a smaller amount—but I had made it a big deal in my own mind.

Was I being rebellious? Was it pride that made me unwilling to go to Bob and simply talk the matter over? Probably the answer was yes to both questions. The sins of pride and rebellion seemed to go together. "Pride goeth before . . . a fall." As if I needed a reminder, the proverb seemed to continually come into my mind.

Morality, someone has said, is the choice between possible courses of action. If my choices only revolved around myself, what decisions would I really be making? I believe that our leaders do what they think is right in making financial requests and issuing Church calls, but desperation can sometimes overrule inspiration—and I knew our ward finances were in trouble. Was it pride that motivated me? Was I too worldly, caught up in "the thick of thin things"?

Pride is a sin of selfishness—self-centeredness, self-satisfaction, self-exaltation—and on selfishness and competition our current society seems based. At work there are so many people who are so agitated with themselves, wondering all the time whether they are fully "actualizing" themselves. Their focus on self-improvement is genuine, but is measured only by how good they feel about themselves. They seem to watch and measure their moods and feelings as much as they do their weight on bathroom scales. They turn to new approaches to look out for number one and be successful as frequently as they search out new diets. Had I too sold my birthright for a mess of pottage and become too much "in the world"?

One of the worst vices a person can have is pride. It was because of pride that Lucifer became the devil. Pride leads to every other vice in some way. C. S. Lewis has noted that the more pride a person has, the more that person dislikes pride in others. He wrote: "If you want to find out how proud you are the easiest way is to ask yourself, 'How much do I dislike it when other people snub me, or refuse to take any notice of me, or shove their oar in, or patronise me, or show off?' . . . Pride gets no pleasure out of having something, only out of having more of it than the next man. We say that people are proud of being rich, or clever, or good-looking, but they are not. They are only proud of being richer, or cleverer, or better-looking than others. . . . Once the element of competition has gone, pride has gone." (*Mere Christianity* [New York: Macmillan, 1943], p. 109–10.)

These thoughts provoked a terrible question. Was I competing with Bob? Was I unwilling to make a commitment to him because I truly down deep inside thought I was better than he was—better educated, more well read in the scriptures, better off financially —and I wasn't going to have him tell me what to do?

I wondered as I prayed that night if I was claiming to be a servant of the Lord but really all the time was imagining that he approved of me and that he surely thought I was far better than other, more ordinary people. I wondered, too, if I was becoming one of those people the Savior spoke of who would testify of him and cast out devils in his name but at the final judgment be told that he had never known them. I am convinced that the Lord has given us a "rule of thumb" to figure out whether pride is too much a dominant influence on us. Whenever we feel that we are "beating" someone else, that we are morally or spiritually superior, we can be certain that pride is at the core. We are being "acted upon" by circumstances rather than humbly choosing to serve the Lord.

I gave some thought then to the idea of humility. To be humble is not to "put yourself down." A false humility is no more to be praised than a false pride. As he leaves the proud in purgatory, Dante is escorted by the Angel of Humility. People describe humility as peace, sweetness, and "a kind of suspension of the heart in a delighted tranquility." There is no need for striving to beat someone else or to do better than someone else. There is no striving to triumph over others, only to see ourselves as we really are—with our own gifts and our own choices to make—not to impress others with our commitment and dedication nor to resist requests simply because we think too much is being asked of us but rather to search our hearts to find the "peace that surpasseth understanding."

I had worked to become well-to-do and successful because that allowed me to feel that I would never have to "do without." I could do almost anything I really wanted to do simply because I could afford it. I was viewing the goal of life as "winning" without giving up anything. Advancement, comforts, education, Church service, temple attendance—I was going to have it all. But as I contemplated that request I could see that it wasn't possible to have it all. I wasn't that good. I couldn't do that much. Maybe others could, but I couldn't. I had some abilities, but my energy level only let me do so much. I could have *anything* I wanted, but not *everything* I wanted. I had to choose. I wondered if

Bob realized that when he made that request for a significant donation to the ward budget for the year. I am sure the Lord knew.

I was invited that Saturday by Larry, an LDS Social Services representative, to a unique workshop he was conducting. He was my friend and said he wanted my views on this little minicourse he was conducting with individuals and couples who were experiencing significant depression. So I went. As we met over the next three weekends it became apparent that the membership of this little group had only one thing in common: their varied dreams—of marriage, health, solvency, popularity, youth, achievement—had all fallen apart, and the shattering of those dreams had broken the dreamers' hearts.

But in spite of the collapse of those dreams Larry helped them gain powerful insights into their own motivations and choices. Rather than relying on their own dreams and their individual talents, they could gain enduring strength through accepting the Savior's dream and the blessings of group camaraderie in the Church. "Where else could you go and be accepted regardless of what you brought with you?" he asked the group members. Each told a different story of broken dreams in that little group, but each also found a new dream to believe in—a dream supplied by the Lord, who said that the last shall be first, that the meek shall inherit the earth, and that a broken heart and a contrite spirit produces the kind of compassion that provides an opportunity to embrace the ultimate dream. Because I became a member of this group rather than a bystander, I changed too. It was as if the wringer on my grandmother's old washing machine in her basement wrung out of me my jealousy and stubbornness as I shared in the dreams and failures of nine others who felt they had nothing else to lose. And I too lost a burden. The hardness and defiance I felt simply drained out of me.

I sat down after the last meeting and drew up a family budget. I included items I thought we needed and those we wanted. I was convinced that the real issue was to make a budget contribution that involved some sacrifice on *my* part. The amount was less important than the process I had gone through in reaching a decision. I had struggled with some feelings unnecessarily, ascribing to others feelings and motives which were not there. I had set up a race course, created a competitive situation that simply wasn't there. But in the process I had learned something about myself and I had become a better person for it. I saw myself more clearly. And in seeing myself I was better able to recognize that I had made a rubber band of the iron rod—stretching it to fit my situation instead of changing my motives and desires to conform to it.

The story is told of a very wise rabbi to whom students often asked penetrating questions. "Rabbi," one said to him, "in the old days there were those who saw God. Why doesn't anybody see God nowadays?"

And the Rabbi replied, "Oh, my son, nowadays no one can stoop so low." Indeed, many of us have a difficult time humbling ourselves enough to begin to understand and approach God. I made a simple decision and it changed my life. I will never be the same again.

I am now convinced that the race does not go to the swiftest or the strongest. Reaching the goal of self-fulfillment and eternal life means being less competitive—being meek and lowly—rather than trying to be the "best" by beating everyone else. "Ye cannot serve God and mammon" (Matthew 6:24) is not just a good moral principle, it is fact. The two cannot be held in tension; one will win out.

By chasing after money and success I had developed a kind of split consciousness in which the Lord was placed in one box and the rest of my life—"reality"—in another. While I had faith in the Savior and even read the scriptures regularly, I was so busy chasing security, wealth, and status that I had little time left over for anything else.

It was only when I critically examined what I said I believed in and where I was spending my time and money that I realized what a hypocrite I was. But at least hypocrites know they should be something more than they are.

13

Karen

I first met Karen after she had been beaten up by her husband and she didn't know where else to go for help. I was the Relief Society president, but since she was completely inactive in the Church she was just another name on the ward roster to me. She was afraid, very afraid, when she called. I was the only reliable resource that she could think of for assistance. She was thirty years old and married for the second time, to a much older man. She was scared that he would seriously hurt her if he came back and simply wanted some advice about what she should do. I drove to her house and entered a world that was as foreign to me as another country. It wasn't the bruises on her arm and shoulder that shocked me. It was the fear. Like a caged and frightened puppy, she sat shivering and anxious while we talked.

She had been dependent on other people all of her life and now didn't know what to do. She was scared to be on her own and was scared about what was going to happen to her.

As we talked about what she should do now, Karen couldn't restrain her tears. She said that others had taken advantage of her throughout her life and that only other women in the Church seemed to be trustworthy to her and that that was why she had called me. She couldn't help telling me about her past. When Karen was just a young teenager, her mother remarried and her stepfather soon afterward began making sexual advances toward her. She resisted but he wouldn't stop. Finally she left home and moved in with friends who were members of the Church. Within a few months she was baptized. But the family she was staying with were struggling financially, and unfortunately she decided to leave them to marry a nonmember. She was only fifteen.

By the time Karen was nineteen years old she had three children and her husband had been sent to prison. At nineteen, with three small children, she was unemployed. Her lack of skills and education made her virtually unemployable. She turned to the state social services agency, who advised her to put her children into foster homes. She was young, inexperienced, and uncertain how she was going to provide for her children. She followed this advice, thinking it would be only a temporary separation. Through a series of events she really didn't understand, her children were permanently taken from her. Later divorced and now remarried, she had a young son for whom she said she would do anything to protect and raise. She had already endured a great deal, it appeared to me.

In the weeks that followed Karen decided to seek a legal separation from her husband. She wanted me to go with her, so I went with her to see her lawyer. I went with her to court. I went with her to ask for a restraining order against her husband. Later we worked together as she found a job. We worked together on baby-sitting and car pool arrangements. She didn't have a driver's license and didn't know how to drive so we practiced together on some back streets in my neighborhood. Although she took me away from my own four young children, I felt a lot of satisfaction in facilitating Karen's personal growth.

Karen's reactivation wasn't viewed universally by all the ward members as a positive event. Several people who had known her years before warned me about her. They said she was probably into drugs and shouldn't be trusted. One of the ward leaders said simply, "She's a bad seed and will eventually turn on you. Whatever you do for her will be wasted."

I'm not sure what I expected from Karen. I didn't want her to "turn out" a certain way, although I was pleased that she was attending church and trying to live the gospel. Mostly I just saw her as someone who needed help. I felt that it wasn't up to me to decide whether or not she deserved my help or deserved my trust or deserved my compassion. I simply could not turn my back on her. She needed me.

When a very kind older sister in the ward came to me privately, looking out for my best interests, to caution me to not get too involved with Karen, I broke down and cried. With tear-stained cheeks I said, "I guess because I see how much I'm needed, I cannot turn my back on Karen. I hope that I can receive as much trust from the Lord as I am giving to Karen. I hope the Lord's compassion for me goes beyond what he knows about my past.'' She cried too, and together we made some plans to go visiting teaching together to Karen's house.

In the months that followed, Karen and I did many things together. She also told me about some of her difficulties and her waywardness. I was shocked and occasionally embarrassed by some of the things she said. She was a very lonely person who seemed unable to find true companionship either inside or outside the Church. I was the only friend she had ever had for more than a few weeks.

Over the next few months she told me a lot of dark secrets, things that had happened to her in the past that helped me understand her negative attitude about religion. She talked about her fears of coming back and her worries about what people would think. She told me of a time when she had been wrongly accused of something she hadn't done and everyone had assumed that she had done it because she had never told anyone anything different.

''So many people believed that I was basically bad that even I was convinced,'' she said.

She didn't know if the Lord would ever forgive her and she wasn't sure she could forgive herself. Yet in spite of her past, I had a warm, sweet feeling. I sensed that our Heavenly Father really cared for her no matter what she had done. He still cared. It was a powerful confirmation of how deeply he cares for each individual no matter what they have done in their lives. After several months she told me she wanted to go to the bishop but would only do so if I would go with her. Eventually arrangements were made to meet with the bishop.

As we sat in the car before going into his office, it was apparent that she was scared. She didn't think he would understand. We prayed together and then went into the bishop's office—together. She told of many different things she had done in her life that she knew were wrong. Some were significant, others were trivial.

Finally she said to him, "I knew when I was doing something that was wrong. But I was afraid to stop living the way I was and return to the Church. Who would accept me? I had already been excommunicated. Besides, I had already lost everything that was important to me, including my children. I didn't have a family at all; I was alone. What did it matter if I did everything that there was to do wrong? Nothing mattered. I didn't matter. That is the only thing I can say to explain all of the terrible things that I have done."

I remember the sweet, warm spirit that filled the room as the bishop got up, came over, held her hands, and said, "Time for you to go on from here. You have made amends. You have been forgiven and the Lord loves you."

I felt a feeling of forgiveness and love emanating from the bishop, a feeling of forgiveness for sins that were unimaginable to me, and I *knew* that she was forgiven by the Lord too. That was real. It wasn't just a nice story about someone I didn't know or couldn't relate to. It was about Karen and she was sitting right here next to me. It felt wonderful.

I know it isn't up to us to decide who deserves compassion or forgiveness. It is only up to the Lord, and he holds that love and compassion and forgiveness for each one of us. Though our sins be as scarlet, after our repentance they become as white as snow.

14

The Secret That Everyone Knew

My name is Beth. I am an alcoholic. I didn't set out to be one, but I am one anyway. My father was an alcoholic and I vowed to myself in growing up that I would not be one. But good intentions aren't good enough. It takes more than willpower to avoid being an alcoholic. In my case, it took more than being baptized into the Church. I wanted to stop drinking—or so I thought—when I joined the Church, but I didn't. Once I took a drink again after being baptized, I turned my life over to events around me and lost my ability to choose for myself.

Looking back on my drinking career, it's difficult to say why I started drinking at all since I had seen its devastating effect on my father. Why does a peson start and keep any bad habit? Drinking is like biting your fingernails: it's hard to say *why* anyone would start it. Without thinking much about it, it can overtake a person and make him a slave. After a while, I didn't decide to take a drink; I was drinking all the time. I was never the get-drunk-and-fall-down-the-stairs type. I drank to relax, to reduce stress, or just to make the cares of the world go away for a little while. It just got out of hand. I hardly knew what was happening to me until it was almost too late to do anything about it.

I first tasted beer as a teenager. I tried it because all my friends were trying it, but I didn't like the taste. Ironically, that's when I met my first Mormon. He was a friend of some of the boys I knew. We even dated a time or two. I didn't know much about his church but I was attracted to him because of the high standards he maintained. I never saw him again after high school.

In college I tried wine and most liquors and eventually developed a taste for various mixed drinks. So what? I knew I was in control as a social drinker. I got married in college, moved to the suburbs when my husband graduated, had two children, and settled down to a middle-class life-style.

Then I came home one evening to a note from my husband. He was tired of the rut he was in and wanted to change his life. He was leaving me. I was bewildered. I wondered what I had done to deserve this. How was I going to take care of two preschoolers? For the first time in my life I bought packaged liquor bottles and took it all home for the express purpose of sitting down and drinking it. By myself. It's easier to feel sorry for yourself when you're drinking alone.

I struggled financially and emotionally for three years trying to make ends meet and be a positive influence on my small children. Then things began looking up. I remarried and found many of my worries fading away. I drank more openly than I had for the past few years, but nobody knew how frequently I was drinking. Not even me. I drank when I was happy—to celebrate. I drank when I was sad—to ease the pain. I drank when I was nervous or stressed—to relax and calm down. I drank on weekends—to enjoy being away from work. I drank on weekdays—to help me until the weekend. Any occasion would do. I always felt I was in control of my drinking and would have been shocked if someone said that I was drinking too much.

Trouble was just around the corner. I lost my job due to a large layoff from work. Without a second income, we couldn't afford our house payments and eventually were evicted amid other legal problems. So of course I turned to drinking for consolation. I couldn't find another job in my field and found it difficult simply to stay home all day. Being a housewife was hard work and not very exciting. Was this all there was to my life? Would we ever find a way out of all the financial debts we had accumulated? Would I find a way to be a success at anything? I kidded myself into thinking that drinking was the only means of getting to an answer. Like a car engine revved up but still in neutral gear, I was all charged up but going nowhere.

After two years of staying at home, staying up late, and drinking alone, I took the first positive step toward controlling my drinking. I signed up for Alcoholics Anonymous. For nine months I regularly attended weekly meetings in three different groups. It was helping, but I felt guilty because of the time away from my family. I should have just cut back on my attendance; instead I dropped out altogether. My drinking went underground when I stopped attending AA meetings. Since by attending them I had admitted I had a problem, it made me feel weak and inadequate that I couldn't just stop. After all, hadn't I attended AA meetings for nine months? What did it take? It took more than everything I had done so far. It's always been difficult for me to talk to anyone about my feelings. Without the encouragement of AA and the openness and non-judgmental atmosphere they fostered, I silently guarded my self-doubts and inadequacies and kept them to myself.

For the next four years I played a deceptive game of hide-and-seek with my family. I used various cooking bottles to hold my favorite alcoholic beverages and used a lot of mouthwash to disguise my drinking. It was a secret which I thought only I knew.

On a hectic day early in 1986 I did something unusual. I was desperate. My life was going nowhere. There had to be something better than this. I knelt down and prayed, "Show me a way out, dear Lord. Lead me out of this mess I'm in. Please help me." A few hours later, two young LDS missionaries stood at my doorstep. I let them in and my family and I took the discussions. Within weeks we were baptized.

As I progressed in the gospel I became more and more firm in my resolve to completely stop drinking. I had stopped for a few months when I was baptized, but as time passed I started drinking again. I prayed for help, but the only thing that really seemed to help me was to have a drink.

I was called as Relief Society secretary and gratefully accepted this calling, knowing that it would put me in regular contact with those women in the ward whom I most admired. I wanted to faithfully fulfill my calling to continue to enjoy the peace and harmony which were obvious in my home since we had joined the Church. I prayed that the Lord would take from me the desire to drink. I wanted to do better, to be better, to be worthy. Somehow, though, I just couldn't stop drinking. It was too much for me.

It was difficult for me to keep drinking and go to church meetings each Sunday. Because I cared for the people in the ward, I could not bear for them to think badly of me. So I told myself that I would take it slowly and cut down gradually. But the harder I tried, the more uptight I became and the more I needed a drink or two to relax me.

I was having a very hard time reconciling my Church ideals with my actions. So I stopped attending church. It was easier to give up prayer, scripture study, and church meetings than drinking. Since I couldn't live with myself and do both, I gave up the Church. After all, hadn't I tried? Didn't I say I would do it if the Lord would only help me? But where was he? He hadn't taken away my desire to drink even though I had prayed that he would. He had let me down.

When I stopped trying to live the gospel things only got worse. My children seemed to fight and bicker more. My husband and I quarreled. I was edgy all the time and, for the first time I can remember, even drinking didn't help. For months, we stayed away from church and avoided contact with Church members whenever possible. But my Relief Society president and our home teachers were too difficult to avoid all the time. They kept inviting us to meetings and outings. Even when we said we would come and didn't, they called us back. In a quiet way, they were relentless.

I didn't know where to turn. I wanted the positive influence of the gospel back in my home, but I didn't want to be a hypocrite. I was too ashamed to talk to anyone at church about it. I didn't want them to think of me as weak and pitiful. Besides, they were all so good and capable and strong; how could they relate to me even if they wanted to? So I shut myself off from the very people who could help me most.

I felt so guilty. I was living a lie. I knew better than to go on drinking the way I was, but I seemed powerless to do anything about it. I was like a car stalled in the middle lane of an expressway: I wasn't moving, but I didn't dare get out, either. I felt too unworthy even to pray and ask for help. I knew I had to make a decision to do something, but I just couldn't come to terms with myself and decide what to do.

Then I had a dream. I was in a city that was celebrating a local event. Everyone was in a festive mood. I was pushed along by the crowd for a while until I came to the front door of a building. Some people in the crowd handed the doorman an invitation and went in, while others were turned away. I felt a great deal of anticipation and wanted to go in. I was shown to a small room off to the side and was told that I had an invitation but that it was not yet available. I could see through a window that outside the crowd was getting unruly. I was anxious to go into the building as soon as possible, but somehow I couldn't. I became frantic. Where was I? Where was my invitation? I wanted it now. Was it lost? Why couldn't I go in if there was an invitation for me? Suddenly I felt my husband shaking me. He had been awakened by my shouting and woke me to get me to calm down. I lay in my bed quivering, staring at the ceiling.

The next day was Sunday and for the first time in months we decided to attend church. The Sunday School lesson was on Lehi's dream. It was my dream too! A crowd pressing forward, finding the right path, then some people getting sidetracked and not being able to make it all the way to the end, not knowing which way to turn. I had started down the right path but had taken a detour and had gotten lost. Now I couldn't seem to find my way back.

I went home and cried. I went into my own bedroom, closed my door, and sobbed for more than an hour. I called my mother and asked her to come and stay with my family for a while. I had made a decision. I was going to check into a substance abuse center for alcoholics.

Eight weeks of individual counseling, group therapy, and personal study can be a long time. But it passed quickly for me. I was able to break away from my daily routine of everyday living and really look at myself in the mirror. I stopped blaming myself, my husband, my children for not being perfect, and I discovered ways to open up and talk to them without hurting their feelings. My family was very supportive and helped me through the embarrassment and shame I felt for not being a better wife and mother.

I wrote a long letter to my bishop. I told him where I was and how badly I felt that I had deceived him about my drinking in the various interviews he had had with me. Later when I talked to him face-to-face and confessed to all my inadequacies, I felt that what mattered the most to him was my future, not my past.

I see myself more clearly today than I ever have in the past. I know my tendencies much better than I ever have. As an alcoholic, I can never be "fixed." The best I can hope for is to live well and to avoid the circumstances that tempt me to drink. Discouragement comes and goes just as it does for others. Now, however, rather than keeping my problems to myself and trying to handle them alone, I think I'm more willing to let others help me and share my burdens. There are some things that just can't be done alone. Many friends in my ward were willing to help me if I was simply willing to include them. It was I who had judged them and worried about what they thought. Since coming back to church I see that I was never really alone.

15

Single-Minded Pursuit

All I want is to be happy! That's all I really want. That doesn't seem like too much to ask, does it? Probably most people would say about the same thing. It has been something I have worked hard to achieve. In spite of that, however, most of my life has been unhappy. Why should that be? If all I ever wanted was happiness, why should it be so difficult to get?

Time and again I've asked myself, Is this what I really want out of life? Is this all there is to it? In all this pursuit of happiness, I have seen the loneliness of looking out for number one. You see, this has a particular meaning to me because I am only twenty-six years old and I am dying. I know I am dying because I have an incurable disease. It is AIDS—Acquired Immune Deficiency Syndrome.

AIDS is a very painful disease. It is the result of my single-minded pursuit of what I once thought was my homosexual nature. For eight years, since I was seventeen years old, I had convinced myself that homosexuality was simply a part of my nature. Whether it was the result of role models in my youth or a biological mistake or something else, it simply was something I thought I could not change. That is a lie.

I know it is a lie because I have changed. I have bloodied and bruised my knuckles by knocking on heaven's gate and have found that with the Lord, truly all things are possible. He has seen my pain, healed the wounds on my soul, and transformed me as a person—as we must each allow him to do for us. In making the necessary changes I have paid an awful price. And although it has been difficult to repent, there is perhaps no happier feeling than knowing I am acceptable to the Lord.

Although I was born under the covenant to parents who were active in the Church, I have not always cared about pleasing the Lord. Sure, I participated fully in Primary and the youth programs while growing up. But when I became a senior in high school, Church activities didn't appeal very much to me. I was tired of all the restrictions in the Church and resentful of people always telling me what to do. My brother was living in Provo at the time and so my parents let me go live with him for my last year of high school, hoping that I would benefit from the strong, positive environment there.

I had grown up very insecure and unsure of myself because I felt I was too thin and unattractive. But in Provo I got a part-time job in a men's store and learned to dress with style. After graduation, I moved to Los Angeles to study marketing in the clothing industry, and I suddenly found an opportunity to do fashion modeling and TV commercials. For someone who had grown up with a poor self-image, feeling too thin and unattractive, this was like a dream come true! I indulged myself completely and tried to be accepted by all the people around me. I was jetted to exotic foreign lands, chauffeured by limousine to black tie dinners; and I began experimenting with champagne, recreational drugs, and homosexuality. It didn't take long for me to become addicted to them all. I was living life in the fast lane and it seemed others were just a little envious of all that I had. I finally thought, *I've got it all —power, money, prestige, recognition. The world is truly my oyster!*

After several years of trying out almost anything I could imagine, I found out that just as roller coaster rides go up, inevitably they also go down. I woke up one morning and realized that work was tapering off, that I owed several thousand dollars on various clothing and restaurant accounts, and that I didn't have much money in the bank. Then the few friends I had began to leave me.

Well, when the work stopped, the dinner invitations stopped, the parties stopped, and many of the people who seemed to be friends disappeared. As a result, I became angry and bitter with the world. The vices of my lifestyle—even if they offered only escape—still seemed to offer more pleasure than anything else.

Not one person around me cared enough to say, "Stop it! You're destroying yourself." Then one day a friend came over to visit and found me locked in my apartment, beaten badly. My jaw had been torn from my face, both of my arms were broken, and I was only semiconscious. To this day, I still don't know who did it or why I was beaten up so badly.

I couldn't have sunk any lower. After the necessary surgery had been done to repair what was possible, I lay in a hospital bed and cried to my Father in Heaven

—my first attempt at prayer in years. "I want to believe in you, dear God," I said. "I want to know the right path. Please, help my unbelief."

A short time after this incident I joined the military forces. I needed some kind of job and some means of livelihood and this was the only option I could think of. It was the best thing that could have happened to me. I was assigned to a unit as a medic and became friends with a faithful, active Latter-day Saint. This was my first real contact with the Church in more than six years. We began to have long discussions and to read the scriptures together. At first I didn't tell him that I was also a member of the Church. I was too embarrassed. But after several months and a couple of missionary discussions, I realized that I must drop my pretenses if I was ever going to make any real progress in the gospel.

I stopped drinking and using drugs but continued in on-again, off-again homosexual encounters. I just couldn't seem to break it off, to really turn from it. I wanted to, I told myself, but I just couldn't. This seemed to be a part of me. *I know the scriptures say it's a sin,* I thought, *but maybe I'm just different. Maybe somehow it's like a birth defect that no one intended to have happen but it just did without it being anyone's fault.*

I was in turmoil. Was I some kind of "Ripley's Believe It or Not," a freak? Had I been made different from everyone else or was I rationalizing my actions? I didn't know what to do or where to turn. No one seemed to have the right answer for me. Normal marital relations may be right for everyone else, but that didn't seem to fit for *me.* I wanted to follow gospel principles but they were just too hard to live.

For the first time in my life, I didn't give up on something that was difficult for me. My life had been a shambles. I had joined the military in penniless desperation. Now, in trying to come back to the Church, I felt that I had found the place where I truly belonged. At least I was trying, though I wasn't completely converted. It was as if I was standing outside my own house with the door locked and the key hidden in a new place. All I needed was to find the key and I would be able to be warm and safe inside. But where was it? Where should I look? I had fasted. I had prayed. But I was not different. Why wouldn't God simply recognize my intentions and carry me the rest of the way?

Over the next several months I felt I truly was trying to do my best. Then unexpectedly I began losing weight. I was diagnosed as having Crohn's disease, a cancer of the colon. Massive steroid therapy was applied, but after six months I was still very ill. The doctors weren't completely convinced of a correct diagnosis and so routine blood work for various more uncommon diseases was arranged. After a few days, small tumors appeared on my legs which were biopsied and came back as Kaposi's sarcoma. I had AIDS.

I was discharged from the military and turned to the one sure place where I knew I would always be welcome: home with my parents. Through all the years, through all the pain, I could still go home.

At first I didn't want anyone to know what was really wrong with me because I didn't want to embarrass my parents further. But I knew I had to go to my bishop and make a full confession to him. As we talked it seemed that all my falsehoods, all my selfishness, all my vindictiveness was being burned away. He asked me if I was angry at the Lord because of my disease and if I was simply making a "deathbed confession." I told him I wasn't angry, although I felt that I had wasted so much of my life. And because I had changed months ago from a loud, boisterous person who demanded to be the center of attention to a more thoughtful, easy-going person who was truly interested in others, I felt I really had become a different person.

Eventually, a bishop's court was held and I was asked to confess my sins once again. After the authorities held an extremely long deliberation, I was called back into the room and given the verdict. No formal action would be taken regarding my membership considering my lack of gospel knowledge during my inactive period. I was shocked. And humbled. *Do they care about me that much?* I thought. *How could they love me that much? How could they trust me to be faithful that much?* I wept for a long, long time. If ordinary people could love me that much, I thought I could understand a little about how much God could love me.

Some months later I was able to receive the Melchizedek Priesthood and be ordained an elder. Although confined to a wheelchair, I have attended the temple as often as my health has allowed.

Although the last year and a half have been excruciatingly painful, they have been the happiest days of my life. Sometimes people say, "If you have your health, you have everything." Well, I don't have my health and yet I do have everything. I have the gospel of Jesus Christ.

I have been in and out of the hospital for several months. There isn't much anyone can do for me. Maybe it's part of my personal atonement for my sins that I must suffer like this for so long. I don't really know. But it doesn't matter. I have already endured a much worse trial. I have forsaken my sins. To know that I have been forgiven and am accepted by the Lord is an incomparable feeling! This disease can never affect that.

Note: Two weeks after losing consciousness at only twenty-six years of age, this temple-endowed priesthood bearer passed away.

16

We Can Change

There is an old story which is told about two travelers who met in the woods. One man approached the other and remarked that he was lost and needed help in finding his way out. The other traveler replied that he too was lost and needed help. Then he said, "We can help each other by telling about the paths we have already tried. That will help us eliminate some and perhaps it will make it easier for us to find our way out."

There are many paths in life. Some are dead ends and provide only disappointment rather than direction. Repentance enables us to recalculate our bearings when we take these false paths and to set a course for a different destination. Sometimes these course changes are minor adjustments and are made periodically to ensure that all is proceeding well. Sometimes they are major revisions when we require significant overhauls to set things straight.

In today's society we don't like to use the word *sin* very often; it makes us uncomfortable. It seems out-of-place, too harsh, too old-fashioned a term. It's often easier to pass off sin as something which affects everyone and then do nothing about the sins that belong to us. As is the case with well-used possessions, sometimes it's easier to simply keep the familiar sins we've grown comfortable with than to repent and change our lives. It's easier to hold a grudge than to try to befriend someone who has offended us. It's easier to criticize a ward leader than it is to go to him and work out a problem. We can ignore our own sins simply by not recognizing them for what they are. On the other hand, we can demolish our self-respect with tortured introspection. Elder Neal A. Maxwell has said: "Self-contempt is of Satan; there is none of it in heaven. We should, of course, learn from our mistakes, but without forever studying the instant replays as if these were the game of life itself." (*Ensign*, November 1976, p. 14.) Nephi noted: "And now, my beloved brethren, seeing that our merciful God has given us so great knowledge concerning these things, let us remember him, and lay aside our sins, and not hang down our heads, for we are not cast off" (2 Nephi 10:20).

We are all tempted. We all have inadequacies. What we do about them matters more than the fact that we have them. A physical body is a delicate instrument. While it can receive promptings from the Holy Ghost, it is also subject to the weakness that mortality brings. In the book of Ether we read that if we will come unto the Lord, he will show us our weakness, our small place in the vast universe of God's creations, a fact which Moses saw, causing him to wonder about mankind's significance. In the book of Ether we also read the Lord's promise that if we come to him he will make weak things strong for us. (Ether 12:27.) By purifying our hearts, we can sit at the Lord's right hand and participate with him in administering the laws and ordinances of the gospel throughout the universe we can see and even in the worlds beyond our view. If we can imagine ourselves in such company and let that perspective guide our actions there will be no doubt as to our exaltation. Creating a visual image of who we are and what we can become is a powerful motivating force which prompts repentance and enables us to feel the healing power of forgiveness.

Through the process of repentance and forgiveness, then, we can feel the relief and subsequent joy of having the burden of our sins lifted. The nature of this burden and its removal has been effectively illustrated in an article from the *Church News*, quoted by President Thomas S. Monson in the April 1988 general conference. The article notes that an oceangoing ship often has hundreds of shellfish known as barnacles which will fasten themselves to the ship's hull, making travel very difficult. Only by docking in a freshwater harbor, the article explains, can the ship rid itself most effectively of these burdensome barnacles. The illustration continues:

> Sins are like those barnacles. Hardly anyone goes through life without picking up some. They increase the drag, slow our progress, decrease our efficiency. Unrepented, building up one on another, they can eventually sink us.
>
> In His infinite love and mercy, our Lord has provided a harbor where, through repentance, our barnacles fall away and are forgotten. (*Ensign*, May 1988, p. 42.)

The restored gospel of Jesus Christ does not impose standards on us in order to create anxiety or frustration when it seems too difficult to follow the precepts of the gospel. Perhaps sometimes we try too hard. Perhaps we spend too much time going places on the open ocean of life when we need simply to rest more in the safe freshwater harbors. A magazine once carried an interview of an eighty-five-year-old woman from the hill country of Kentucky. Asked to reflect on what she would do over again if she could redo her life she said, "I would relax. I would be sillier, I would take fewer things seriously. . . . I would eat more ice cream and less beans. I would perhaps have more actual troubles, but fewer imaginary ones. . . . You see, I've been one of those people who never went anywhere without a thermometer, a hot water bottle, a raincoat, and a parachute. If I had to do it again, I'd travel lighter."

In a world where few of us will do great deeds that cause someone to congratulate us from the podium, the Lord has nonetheless given us the capacity to find greatness in everyday living. We can do the good that lies within our power, and we should know that if we do our best it will be good enough. The Lord sees us so clearly that he knows better than anyone else our sorrows and disappointments, our temptations and sins, and he can forgive us and eventually cause even us to forget them.

Because of his great love for us, our Father in Heaven has provided a way for us to become free from the effects of sin and to receive total and complete forgiveness. Just as sin can darken our spiritual nature, so can repentance lighten our spirits and our lives. It is a great gift available to all who choose to seek it.

We may sometimes think that we are not capable of changing, that changing is just too hard, that our weaknesses are either too small and not worth the effort or too large and not possible to alter. At some time in our lives, we probably recognize that we cannot simply change by our own efforts alone.

Repentance, of course, is more than personal change. It is more than just deciding to do things differently and then gritting our teeth until we achieve our goals. If we will yield our hearts to the Lord, he will change them. It is as simple as that. This does not imply that it is easy to change; usually it is very difficult to do so, for we must peel away years of entrenched habits or give up cherished biases and prejudices. Also, we may have to go through much suffering in order to repent of our sins. But the process itself is simple. It is a simple matter to yield our hearts to the Lord and allow the effects of the Atonement to apply to us individually.

After hearing King Benjamin speak, his people wanted to experience such a change and remarked, "O have mercy, and apply the atoning blood of Christ that we may receive forgiveness of our sins, and our hearts may be purified" (Mosiah 4:2). By turning to the Lord, they discovered that he had "wrought a mighty change in us, or in our hearts, that we may have no more disposition to do evil, but to do good continually" (Mosiah 5:2).

Most of us will likely not have a dramatic change of heart that occurs in a single moment. But day by day we can work to give our hearts to the Lord. By doing so, we can begin to feel as he feels, and we will want to act as he has counseled us to act. We will have no desire to sin. We will know the overwhelming joy and miracle of forgiveness.